7 Lessons for Success

for Success

My Mother's Guide to What Really
Works in Life and Business

Audrey

To your Success!

Fusion 2019

Also Published by Zan Monroe

Stories of Uncle Adrian: A Guide to Mastery in Your Life

Audio Productions by Zan Monroe

7 Lessons Every Entrepreneur Should Learn
Build a Business for Life
How the Mind Works
Creating Wealth Through Real Estate
The Perfect Real Estate Day
The World's Greatest Listing Presentation
Absorption Rate Pricing and Positioning

7 Lessons for Success
Published by:
The Monroe Company, Inc.
P.O. Box 58241, Fayetteville, NC 28305
910-624-7100
Zan@ZanMonroe.com
www.ZanMonroe.com

7 Lessons for Success

My Mother's Guide to What Really Works in Life and Business

Zan Monroe

Foreword by Cameron Monroe

This book is dedicated to my mother,
Mary Cornelia Williams "Honey" Monroe
who gave us the gift of
reason, purpose and self-esteem.

Published by:
The Monroe Company, Inc.
P. O. Box 58241
Fayetteville, NC 28305
www.ZanMonroe.com

Cover and interior text design by Rose Gurganious Spell
ISBN: 978-0-9779014-1-8
Library of Congress Control Number: 2016909157

7 Lessons for Success

First Edition
Printed and bound in the United States of America

Table of Contents

Foreword by Cameron Monroe... ix
Introduction by Zan Monroe.. xiii

Lesson 1: Your Best Investment Is Yourself.........................1
• The Bookmobile is Here!..3
• Scraps of Paper...7
• Teaching Mama to Swim..12
• Lost in the Paris Airport..16
• Kaboom!...20
• Mowing the Ditch..24
• Plateau Learning...28

Lesson 2: A Man's Mind Is Like A Garden.........................33
• Philosophy – Who Needs It?...35
• A Man's Mind is Like a Garden...39
• Root Bound..44
• Reason, Purpose and Self-Esteem......................................47
• I Do Not Choose to be a Common Man.................................50
• Cutting Down the Sweet Gum Tree......................................53

Lesson 3: Do What You Enjoy; You Will Be Good At It........57
• Downy Duck Learns to Fly..59
• Do What You Enjoy; You Will Be Good at It..........................64
• I Don't Want to Go to School...67
• Stealing Dogwoods...72
• Your "Is Done" Pile..77
• Raining Rabbits...82
• Cleaning the Gutters..86

Lesson 4: How Money Works..91
• Money Is… 93
• Poor, Rich and Wealthy People..99

- Haircuts on the Porch..102
- Mother's Coconut Cake 107
- Debt is Constant, Income is Variable...............................112
- The Taxman Cometh..116

Lesson 5: Free Minds and Free Markets Create Wealth......123
- The Little Red Hen..125
- Blueprint for a Free Society..133
- A Ticket and Two Flat Tires..139
- A Gardener Needs Seeds... 145
- Food Tastes Better at Honey's House.................................148
- You Might Be a Redneck Capitalist....................................152
- Free Minds and Free Markets Create Wealth..........................156

Lesson 6: Profit Is Better Than Wages.................................163
- Profit is Better than Wages...165
- The Daylily Business.. 171
- Taken to Jail for Playing Tennis...176
- Free Ice Cream Marketing...182
- The Blackbird Theory of Business..185
- Fertilize Before the Rain.. 190
- Watering Holly Bushes...192

Lesson 7: Real Estate Is The Only <u>REAL</u> Investment..........195
- What Would You Buy with $25,000?....................................197
- Money Does Grow on Trees...202
- Moving a House...206
- There is Gold in that House...211
- The Best Time to Plant a Shade Tree....................................216
- Real Estate is the Only <u>REAL</u> Investment............................220
- Tax Sheltered Real Estate Investments.................................223

Did They Get It?...228
Appendix...231
A Dragon Story..237

FOREWARD

It is often said that the first thing to be forgotten of a loved one, after they have passed on, is their voice; the way they speak, how they hang on certain words, and the cadence in which they present their sentences. In some cases this may be true. There are some whose voices I have forgotten, but in reference to my grandmother, this is simply not true.

Known to her grandchildren simply as "Honey," her tones were such that cannot be forgotten. It was a simple voice, seemingly meek to those who paid it little mind. But with further attention, one could sense a deep confidence in the voice of this small, yet resolute woman. Distinct in its sound, I have never known someone to speak as she does. Walking alongside her in her precious garden, I would listen, as she would speak to the nature around her, talking as if the trees and the flowers knew her every word, or reading aloud her beloved books, gleaning as much possible knowledge from the script she was currently indulged in. Rifling through tens of pages at a time, my sister and I would sit, captivated on her living room floor, our ears trained to receive the message she so sweetly provided. Her words came with an unparalleled sense of peace, and were quick to ease those around her. A woman most would miss, if not looking for her, but was heard as if a Queen speaking from her throne. Her voice dripping with experience and knowledge, she could not help but be heard.

I was fortunate to spend the little time I had with her. I was merely seven years old when she passed, but Honey had a greater impact on my life than she, or I, ever realized. At the ripe age of eighty, she was consumed with getting as much as she could out of the life she had left. And my, did she live; raising a family of four after her husband had passed away, turning her love of gardening into a thriving business and spending her days doing exactly as she wished. Strong, yet loving, she carried out those days looking forward to leaving behind a legacy she could be proud of, and a memory that would remain in the minds of those close to her.

A particular instance comes to mind, as I was a young boy, spending time in her home. It was a quaint country home, nestled in the curve of Cloverfield Lane, a home that seemed to transcend the times come before, yet not stuck in the past from whence it came. I was a very inquisitive child, and I often found myself in places, or doing things, that were not always to the liking of the elders around me. On this afternoon, I found myself sitting on the seat of an antique spinning wheel, one that was no doubt far older than I was, and honestly, much more valuable. Clearly handcrafted, I was always intrigued with the contraption and admired the detail and precision with which it was made. Sitting on the attached seat, I began to spin the wheel as quickly as I possibly could, attempting to figure out what the purpose of it was. In my self-entertainment, I did not hear my grandmother enter the room. She walked with a light gait about her, much younger and more graceful than her age should have allowed. I immediately stopped the wooden wheel in my hands, knowing a scolding would soon follow. To my surprise, it did not. She spoke calmly to me; simply stating, "I keep that wheel as a reminder. A reminder of the years past and how far I have come. The hard work that made me who I am, and has allowed you to be who you are." With those words, she turned and quietly exited the sunlit sitting room just as quietly and gracefully as she had entered.

It has taken me until the age of twenty-one to understand what she meant and the pride in which she said them. It was not a self ish statement; simply one to teach and to educate

Mother, Liz, Cornelia and Zan
1965

one who may not have understood the value of the spinning wheel in question. *That is how a life should be spent; in constant education.* Learning what makes the world the way it is and knowing how to handle whatever may come with life, both good and bad. Some people go through their entire lives and never understand this; that to truly live is to gain something every day, to grow as a person in order to make the world a better place.

That's how my Honey lived, as if every conversation, every meeting, and every word were a chance to learn. Clinging to these opportunities like the flowers she dearly loved, waiting for the opportunity to blossom into the most beautiful of blooms possible, brightening the dreariest of lives with a little more color and a great deal more of hope.

Cameron Monroe

Mary & L. A. Monroe
Easter Sunday 1940

INTRODUCTION

"Two roads diverged in a wood and I –
I took the one less traveled by.
And that has made all the difference."
Robert Frost, <u>The Road Not Taken</u>

Her name was Mary Cornelia Williams Monroe and she took the road less traveled. That choice made all the difference in her life and in the lives of everyone around her.

Born January 4, 1917, Mary was the second child of Gus and Maggie Williams. Her parents, grandparents and five siblings all lived in a small brown, three bedroom house on a 110 acre farm in Eastern North Carolina. Their community was called Eastover because it was "east over the Cape Fear River" from Fayetteville, North Carolina.

She started school at the age of five, walking two and a half miles to Eastover School with her brothers and sisters. I would love to say she walked in the snow, uphill in both directions, but the terrain was flat and it seldom snows in Eastern North Carolina. After her first year of school, there was a school bus to carry them every day.

She was twelve years old when the Great Depression hit in October of 1929. The stock market crash marked the beginning of a decade of high unemployment, poverty, low profits and plunging farm incomes. The Williams family grew everything they needed to survive on their farm, earning just enough to pay their property taxes. Living through the depression had a lasting impact on Mary's life, making her acutely aware of how dependent our economic system is on the entrepreneurs who create wealth.

Family life was difficult in the early 1900's. The six children worked hard on the farm, learning a great work ethic from their Scottish parents. Mary learned the value of money at an early age by gathering and selling guinea eggs to a restaurant in town. Ten cents a dozen for eggs was a lot of money for a young girl during the Great Depression.

After graduating high school, Mary got a job as a hairdresser, working for Mrs. Carson's Beauty Shop in Fayetteville. Mary learned how to cut and style hair while Mrs. Carson taught her how to deliver great customer service and maintain a repeat business.

As a repeat customer herself, Mary ate lunch every day at Horne's Drug Store in downtown Fayetteville. Her waitress was a young lady named Mary Belle Monroe who introduced Mary to her brother L.A. The first time he saw Mary, he said she was the most beautiful woman he had ever seen. Because he had a car, L.A. was able to drive to the Williams family home in the country. Mary and L.A. spent many summer evenings sitting on the front porch of that brown country house, accompanied by her five brothers and sisters, as well as her parents. Eventually L.A. proposed and they were married on June 23, 1939, at 10:00am at the Fayetteville Methodist circuit parsonage, by the Rev. J.C. Williams.

In 1943, their first daughter, Mary Alexandra, was born followed by Cornelia Ann and Elizabeth King. Finally in 1955, I was born. They named me Leonidas Alexander Monroe, Jr. but thankfully they called me Zan.

In 1952, our young family moved to Dunn, North Carolina where Daddy opened the Jewel Box store selling jewelry, fine china and clocks. Mama did not work outside the home, but did what most women of that age did, she stayed home and raised her family. Five years later, Daddy sold the Jewel Box and our family moved back to a forty acre section of the original Williams family farm and built a house large enough to raise four children.

Mother ran the house and named our farm "Cloverfield" from a story she read in a children's book. Daddy planted red topped clover in the front pasture to complete the storybook picture. At Cloverfield Farm there were horses, cows, dogs and cats to feed, plus lots of grass to mow. There were party line telephones, clotheslines, homemade blackberry jelly and vegetables from the garden. We ate great food out of the garden like tomato sandwiches on Wonder White Bread with salt, pepper and Duke's Mayonnaise. The black and white television had to warm up before watching and the dishes were washed by hand after every meal. Clothing was cotton and had to be sprinkled with liquid starch and ironed before wearing. Sundays were spent at Salem United Methodist Church, and afterward we were served a large home cooked lunch at the family's Lazy Susan dinner table. We went to the same school that Mama went to when she was young. Life was good for the Monroe family.

Daddy became a builder, working with my Uncle Don to build

houses and King George Apartments with Uncle Adrian. He built Kings Shopping Center on a big tract of land he inherited from his uncle on Bragg Boulevard, the major thoroughfare leading into Fort Bragg. Kings Shopping Center held many stores including the first A&P Supermarket in the region, Gaylord Department Store, the first Krispy Kreme Doughnuts and an Esso gas station.

In the summer of 1965, I was ten years old and our family took a two week vacation driving the family station wagon from North Carolina to Maine and back. We crossed the Chesapeake Bay Bridge Tunnel, toured Washington D.C., Cape Cod, Plymouth Rock, the Mayflower, Philadelphia and the Liberty Bell. In Vermont we ate maple sugar candy, saw the Amish in Pennsylvania and went to the World's Fair in New York City. This was the first time I had left the farm to see our great country.

We stopped at motels along the way, got a key and inspected the rooms before Mother would let us stay the night. Sometimes she gave the key back and we went on to another motel. It was a great two weeks spent traveling, learning and exploring the big world outside our farm. It was also the last trip I would ever take with my Father.

My father had been a smoker since the age of fifteen, but quit smoking in 1964, when the Surgeon General's report was released, linking cigarette smoke to cancer. A couple of months after our vacation, Daddy and I were cleaning out a moldy feed bin in the barn and he began to cough. After a series of tests and x-rays, the doctors determined that he had a mass in one of his lungs about the size of a donut. It was lung cancer. The doctors did surgery,

xvi

radiation and chemotherapy. He died on January 31, 1966, just 90 days after the first diagnosis.

At the age of forty nine, Mary Monroe found herself with three children at home, a forty acre farm to run, partial interest in Kings Shopping Center and King George Apartments and money from life insurance. What she didn't know was what to do with all of it. She had a high school education, no business training and no knowledge of investments. With all her responsibilities, she had no opportunity to work outside the home or go back to school.

Death often leaves you no other option but to make choices and live with the consequences. My father's death forced Mother to make choices to grow and change. She had no choice except to learn, grow and succeed for herself and her children. Mother

"Death often leaves you no other option but to make choices and live with the consequences."

was very afraid of failing, but courage is taking action even when you are afraid. Mother knew that she could not walk away from her responsibility because, as she put it, "I brought you into this world and I am responsible for you."

With her husband gone, Mary realized that no one was coming to rescue her. She had to depend upon and believe in herself, learn how her mind worked, how to think critically and reason logically. She had to discover how businesses operated, how finance worked and how to create wealth. She had to acquire a philosophy of success and she had to inspire and nurture her children to live a successful life. Mother knew she had to choose the road less traveled that would lead her family to emotional, spiritual and financial success. Heroes have the courage to do whatever is necessary in a crisis. Mother became our family's hero.

In Mother's bedroom there was a chair that sat beside the window where she could look out to see an old Magnolia tree and smell the hyacinth's that she planted under the window. After Father died, she would sit by that window and read. She read books on economics, philosophy, religion, government and business. She read books by Thomas Jefferson, Norman Vincent Peale, Dale Carnegie, Ayn Rand and Milton Freedman. She read anything that would guide her spiritually, philosophically and financially to success (see appendix for a complete list).

Mother's given name was Mary Cornelia Williams Monroe and she was called Mary her entire life until her first grandchild, Clay Wade changed her name to Honey.

When Clay was about a year old, his mother went back to her job as a school teacher and Clay got to stay with his grandmother. Every morning when Clay arrived at his grandmother's home, she would prepare him a breakfast of brown bread with butter and honey.

One day as she was sitting at the breakfast table with Clay in her lap while he ate his breakfast, she asked, "You call your other grandmother, Granny. What are you going to call me?" His response was, "I'm going to call you, Honey," meaning the honey on his bread. Immediately the name stuck. It didn't take long for it to spread to the rest of our family and then into the surrounding community. Soon everyone simply knew my mother as Honey Monroe.

Honey did what very few women raised in the south in the early 1900's did; she challenged the stereotype of the day by becoming an independent woman, entrepreneur, philosopher and matriarch of her family. Mother became disciplined in her life, her body, her thinking, her finances and business. She studied philosophy and challenged the conventional thinking of the church. She started numerous businesses, developed land, moved houses and renovated them. Mother learned how to refinish furniture and she collected and sold antiques with my sister in a little business they called "Log Cabin Antiques." Mother loved to landscape yards which she did for herself, her children and neighbors. She subdivided part of our farm to create a neighborhood. She grew flowers for her own pleasure and sold them, too. She traveled the United States, Europe, Hawaii, the Caribbean, Asia and China. She became a force to be reckoned with in the male dominated Republican Party in Eastern North Carolina. She worked to secure a spiritual, educational and financial future for her family.

Mother had a passion for life that endures. She added to the total life on this planet through all the plants she cultivated. She added value to the life of others by sharing her knowledge, philosophy and guidance. She lives today in every bush, tree, flower, and blade of grass that she grew and every person she influenced along her path.

Mother celebrated life every day. She believed in living life to its fullest and living minute by minute. Life lived for the sheer joy of living. Life lived for the joy it brings every day, not the stale promises of an uncertain future. She lived her life based on integrity, wholeness and holiness. She lived her life to create more value in everything she did. She believed in living life, here... now!

She learned to live her life based on the principals of *reason, purpose and self-esteem,* not self-sacrifice. Mother believed that reason is your only tool of survival and that you should use your mind every day to its highest ability. She believed your highest purpose is to continue to expand and grow your intellect daily. She believed that purpose was your choice of achievement in life, which brings happiness. A life lived without purpose is not a life that is lived to its fullest potential. She did not want anyone to waste a single moment of their precious life. She learned that self-esteem is the knowledge that you are worthy of a life filled with joy and happiness. She knew that self-esteem is necessary to live life to its fullest.

Mother knew what it took to create life both in her garden and in her family. She did not seek God with song and ceremony but with a shovel and a wheelbarrow and the dirt that she made from compost.

She loved the story about the scientists who challenged God to a contest. They said, "We are so advanced now that we can make a man out of the dirt of the earth and would like to challenge you to a contest."

God accepted their challenge and said, "OK, but first you have to make your own dirt!"

Honey made her own dirt.

As a child, I often wondered what God looked like. I envisioned a huge bearded man with flowing robes in the heavens looking down upon me. As I have matured, God has come to look more like a gentle woman working in her garden.

From the age of eleven to twenty-one, I learned and grew along with Mother. I read the books she read and attended the lectures she attended. I started businesses and worked alongside her when she developed land, renovated houses, planted gardens and refinished furniture. Her journey took ten years to complete and by 1975, she reached a state of harmony in her spirit, her philosophy and her finances. She was at peace with her life.

A life worth living is a life worth recording. This book is a celebration of Mary Monroe's life and what that life meant. Every person's life leaves a mark on the world, a mark that will make a difference in the lives of everyone they come in contact with. Every person's life is a reflection of their family and its values, the books they read and the thoughts they pass on.

The lessons that are contained in this book are the seven major lessons that Mother learned, adopted and taught me on her journey. If you learn the lessons she taught, read the books she read and travel the road she followed, you will grow a successful life. If you are searching for success and harmony in your life, please allow my mother, Mary Cornelia Williams "Honey" Monroe, to guide you toward a life of spiritual, emotional, philosophical and financial success.

Mother took the road less traveled; the road to success. You can take that road too!

LESSON 1

Your Best Investment
Is Yourself

Mary Monroe and Zan cruise the Caribbean 1967
(Love those shorts!)

The Bookmobile Is Here!

"A person who does not read is the
same as a person who cannot read."
Mary Monroe

"The bookmobile is here. Let's go!" Mother shouted from under the carport. "It is time to go. NOW!" When Mother's voice had that "NOW" tone in it, you dropped whatever you and the dog were doing in the back yard and ran.

The bookmobile brought library books to people who lived in the country, stopping at designated houses once a month. For us kids, the bookmobile was a big event, so when it arrived at Aunt Margaret's house, we all piled in the car and drove over to get a book. Besides, the bookmobile was air conditioned and in the hot North Carolina summer that was a treat. Mother would not take us to the main library in town for fear that we might "wreck the place." Besides, gasoline was twenty-five cents per gallon and that would have been a waste of money.

We had a two-book limit for each child, but Mother checked out as many books as she could read. She was a big reader. A stack of books always sat by her chair and she read constantly. She didn't read fiction; the stack by her chair was composed of books on business, finance, philosophy, religion, and wealth building.

Mother read a book every week of her adult life. Mother's reading and learning meant survival for our family after Daddy died. If you want to improve your life, start by reading some of Mother's favorite books:

As a Man Thinketh, by James Allen
The Power of Positive Thinking, by Norman Vincent Peale
How to Win Friends and Influence People, by Dale Carnegie
Success through a Positive Mental Attitude, by Napoleon Hill and W. Clement Stone
The Richest Man in Babylon, by George S. Clason
The Greatest Salesman in the World, by Og Mandino
Think and Grow Rich/The Law of Success, by Napoleon Hill
The Psychology of Self Esteem/Six Pillars of Self Esteem, by Nathanial Brandon
Capitalism and Freedom, by Milton Friedman
Atlas Shrugged/Capitalism; The Unknown Ideal, by Ayn Rand
Rich Dad Poor Dad, by Robert T. Kiyosaki

Although many people in Mother's generation did not have the chance to go to college, they knew their mind was their only tool of survival, so they read. Today, in our rapidly changing world, just keeping up means you have to learn something new every day. Reading is one of the best ways to learn. Mother's generation read and reread books to extract and digest every bit of information they could. Today, most people don't read with the same depth and attention of earlier generations because there is so much information bombarding us from every direction.

Just because the internet is available with unlimited *information* does not mean that you have knowledge. Information is not *knowledge.* True knowledge comes from using your mind to its fullest every day by assimilating information and converting it into action. That's not an instant process; it's an ongoing process and requires great personal discipline.

In my consulting and speaking business I have the opportunity to work with the top executives of some of the world's largest companies. I deal with some of the most highly educated people in the world, running some of the most successful businesses in the world. When I meet an executive, CEO, or president of a corporation, I can tell immediately if he or she is a reader. Readers are conditioned to constantly learn and expand their minds. They have an unmistakable attitude of openness to new ideas.

> *"A person who does not read is the same as a person who cannot read."*
> Mary Monroe

Mother taught us to read competitively. In business I have learned that new knowledge gives you a competitive edge. If you read one hour a day, you could read an entire book each week. In a year you will have read fifty books; at the end of ten years, five hundred books. If you read that many books based on your industry, you will gain knowledge far beyond your competitors. In today's competitive world, knowledge can be the difference between success and failure.

I tell my clients the same thing Mother told me. *"A person who does not read is the same as a person who cannot read."*

When Mother was eighty-five, macular degeneration set in. Macular degeneration clouds the center of the eye preventing the sight of fine details. Mother lived alone and we did not realize how bad her sight had become. She knew where everything was and still worked in the yard, so it came down to a sense of feel in the end. She had peripheral vision, but could no longer see well enough to read. My mother still wanted to read, learn and grow so my sisters ordered audio books from the North Carolina Association of the Blind.

When my children and I visited, we would often find Mother sitting in her big blue chair listening to an audio book. On more than one occasion she fidgeted around and finally said, "Are you going to be here a while? I'm at a real good place in this book and I would like to finish this chapter. Can you take the kids outside to play and give me just a few more minutes?" And out we would go.

Mother spent a great deal of her time listening to audio books. After she died, the North Carolina Society for the blind sent a letter that said, "In the last 18 months of her life, Mary Monroe read four hundred audio books!"

So congratulate yourself! By reading this book, you have realized the value of one of Honey's lessons and followed her example. She would be proud of you. More importantly, you should be proud of yourself.

Scraps of Paper

"Thinking is hard work. That is why so few people do it."
Mary Monroe

In the early morning, I would find Mother sitting by the window in her bedroom reading. She would stop and say, "Let me read this to you." She would read a powerful statement about life, business, philosophy or religion from whatever book she was currently studying. That statement would not mean very much to me as a young boy, but it obviously meant something to her. She would write the statement on a piece of paper in her sweeping cursive handwriting, fold it carefully, and put it in her pocket. Then she would say, "Let's go work in the yard!" with the same enthusiasm as if she was saying, "Let's go to the county fair!"

We would work in the yard cutting, raking and mowing until we were tired, and then Mother would take a break. She would pull that piece of paper out of her pocket and read it while she strolled around and looked at her work. Sometimes she would stare off into space like she was looking at a great work of art in a museum. She was actually thinking deeply about the powerful statement on her scrap of paper.

She would carry that scrap of paper with her, sometimes for days, taking the time to stop and read that sentence again and again. Once she had internalized that statement she would find another sentence she liked, write it on another scrap of paper and the process would begin all over again. Slowly those powerful statements on little scraps of paper became part of who she was.

Reading those statements changed her beliefs, new beliefs changed the way she thought, and new thoughts changed her actions. Different actions changed her life! She was cultivating the seeds of a better life within her own mind just like she cultivated the seeds of the young plants in her garden.

Mother taught that creating success in your life is as simple as planting a seed in her garden. Every successful activity is first a creative idea. The way your mind creates anything is to first imagine it. Nothing ever gets accomplished without imagination. Imagination is the fine art of creating images within your own mind. These thoughts become the seeds of ideas that will grow in your life. Once you can see an idea clearly, it will take root and grow in your mind and in your life.

Sometimes on Sunday mornings we would all pile in Mother's bed and listen to Dr. Norman Vincent Peele on her big brown radio. If we could talk Mama into listening to him, we didn't have to go to church, so we listened intently. Dr. Peele was the pastor of Marble Collegiate Church in New York City. He wrote *The Power of Positive Thinking* in 1952, and opened a new way of thinking for Mother and an entire generation. Peele was part of the self-help movement of the 1960's and he correlated passages from the Bible. He taught that, if you change your thinking, you can change your life. *The Power of Positive Thinking* taught you how to think correctly, imagine what you want and visualize a successful future. He promoted a philosophy of living to your fullest potential by using affirmations. Affirmations are auto-suggestions from your conscious mind to your non-conscious mind. Peale called using affirmations, "The Law of Auto Suggestion."

His book was one of the first books that helped Mother achieve self-esteem. Mother's scraps of paper with great statements on them were actually affirmations.

Peele taught that you attract into your life whatever you are focused on. Affirmations work on positive or negative statements equally well. In my classes, I teach that whatever you focus on will be incorporated into your beliefs, good or bad. The things you fear will be attracted into your life just as fast as the things you desire. The more you focus on something the larger it becomes in your life. *The good news is, what you focus on expands. The bad news is, what you focus on expands.* When you wander around your house saying, "I cannot find my car keys. My car keys are lost," you are practicing affirmations that prevent you from finding your keys. You should be saying, "I am finding my keys. I remember where I put them and I will see them immediately."

But visualization is only part of the solution. You have to take action. Turning your vision into action is what separates dreamers from doers. Or, as Mama would say, "You have to get off your rear end and do something with your life."

Over time, your thoughts are incorporated into your beliefs. Your beliefs drive your actions. Your actions create the results you have in your life today. If you want to have a different life, you must think differently. Think differently and you will get different results.

Your non-conscious mind stores your beliefs and runs your

life based on those beliefs. Acceptance of any statement as truth incorporates it into your belief system. Your non-conscious mind does not question your beliefs; it simply runs your life based on the beliefs that you have accepted. Your job throughout life is to consciously monitor the things you accept as truth and to be ruthlessly honest with yourself and check all your beliefs against reality. We have absolute control over what reaches our non-conscious mind. Your conscious mind is the gatekeeper to your non-conscious mind.

Over time, Mother's powerful statements changed her beliefs from self-doubt and fear to self-confidence and productive action. She moved from believing she was unworthy of happiness into a powerful, assertive woman. She rejected the philosophy that women were second-class citizens and went on to start businesses and become a powerful civic and political leader. She became an independent thinker by using affirmations. She changed her thinking and changed her life with those little scraps of paper.

Mother's scraps of paper were affirmations that helped change her belief system and move her along the journey toward self-esteem and a more successful life. This book is filled with affirmations just like the ones Mother wrote on her scraps of paper. You can begin to grow a new belief system right now by taking a powerful positive statement from this book, writing it on a scrap of paper and reviewing it often throughout the day. Read it and reread it over and over again until you have planted that statement as a belief in your mind. Then repeat the process by finding another statement that is emotionally powerful, positive and speaks to you of a future you would like to have. Mother was a woman whose life and dreams were changed in a ninety day period follow-ing the death of her husband. Instead of hanging her head and giv-ing up, she took charge. She took the steps necessary to succeed.

Thinking is hard work. That is why so few people do it. To change your life, create a list of positive statements or affirma-tions and spend thirty minutes every day reading and repeating them. It does not have to be thirty minutes at one time; in fact, a much more effective way is to do what Mother did and read them several times during the day. Meaningful repetition is the key to incorporating affirmations into beliefs. Emotions help plant beliefs deeper and more quickly into your mind. By reviewing a powerful and positive statement several times a day you will plant that belief into your mind like a seed that will germinate and grow.

> *"Thinking is hard work.*
> *That is why so*
> *few people do it."*
> Mary Monroe

Planting positive thoughts in your non-conscious mind is just like planting seeds in your garden. When you change your thoughts, you change your beliefs. When you change your be-liefs, you change your actions. When you change your actions, you change your life. Plant more positive thoughts in your mind's garden every day. Read your powerful positive statements to your children, and then take them outside to work in the yard!

Remember what my mother said, *"Thinking is hard work. That is why so few people do it."*

Teaching Mama to Swim

"You can fix just about anything
with vegetables and exercise."
Mary Monroe

Mother had a swimming pool built in our back yard after Daddy died. She knew that regular exercise and proper diet was the way to gain control over her life, and it was also a great way to keep her children occupied during the summer. We swam in the pool a lot the first few years, but then the entertainment value wore off and other interests took over, so we used it less and less.

By the time I was fifteen, I rarely swam in our pool and my older sisters were either married or in college so the pool sat idle most of the time. The year I turned fifteen, Mother said I had to get a job or start a business. In the fall of that year, I enrolled in a Red Cross Senior Life Saving course and during the winter I took a Water Safety Instructor course which certified me to life guard and teach swimming lessons. By the next summer, with Mother's encouragement, I started my first business in our back yard swimming pool. The problem facing me was I had never actually taught anyone to swim. I had all the knowledge but not the experience. Mother wanted to be my first student. She was fifty-five years old and had never learned to swim.

Mother said, "Zan, if you can teach me to swim, you can teach anyone!"

Mother showed up for her first swimming lesson wearing a

large straw hat because she did not want to get her hair wet. I explained to her that she had to get her hair wet to learn to swim, but once she knew how to swim, she could keep her hair dry. She took off her hat and got into the pool with the agreement that this would be the only day she had to get her hair wet.

Mother said she only had thirty minutes for the swim lesson. In the classes I took from the Red Cross we were taught that it took twelve hours to teach someone to swim, so I was faced with the daunting task of not only teaching Mother to swim, but also doing it in thirty minutes.

I skipped a lot of the Red Cross safety information and went right to teaching Mother to swim. To both our surprise, Mother was swimming across the pool in just a few minutes. By the end of the 30-minute lesson she could swim from one end of the pool to the other. I showed her how to swim with her head out of the water, so her hair would not get wet. She said I was a "fabulous swimming teacher."

Mother knew if I could teach her to swim, it would give me the confidence to teach others. Since that day, I have taught hundreds of people to swim, some as young as two years old and many of them adults. I became an expert in teaching adults to swim in just a few minutes. I spent fifteen years teaching swimming every summer because Mother encouraged me by saying, "If you can teach me to swim, you can teach anyone."

Once Mother learned to swim, she swam every day for the exercise. She would work in the yard chopping, shoveling and lifting until she got hot. Then she would cool off by swimming in the pool. She read books on nutrition and ate a very healthy diet and made sure her children did, too. Mother's health was important to her because with her husband gone, she was the only link to a safe and secure future for her children.

Mother believed that you can fix anything with vegetables and exercise. If you want to improve your health and happiness and gain control over your life, start by gaining control over your body. Mother knew that your own body is the only thing you really have total control over. Only you can regulate how much exercise you get and what you eat.

I have interviewed thousands of people who are in stressful situations in life or business and ask them, "What is the best way to relieve stress?" The overwhelming answer is EXERCISE! A simple walk around the block, jog to the corner or workout in a gym is the very best way to reduce stress and live longer. You will also set a great example for your children to follow.

As a professional athlete, I learned that exercise eliminates anger and depression. If you are feeling down or blue, simply get moving! You will discover that exercise is the world's greatest pill for curing whatever ails you. *If you are struggling to gain control over your life, first seek control over your physical body.*

Here are Mother's simple rules for a healthy life and the happiness that comes with it.

1. Exercise at least one hour every day. If you have not exercised

in a while, start with ten minutes of exercise every morning and night and work your way up to one hour.

2. Spread your exercise throughout the day. It doesn't have to be done all at once. Walking is a great exercise and is a good place to start.

3. Eat a diet rich in vegetables, beans, fruits, grains, nuts, fish and olive oil.

4. Avoid animal fat and sugar.

5. Avoid all kinds of fast food.

6. Don't drink soft drinks and limit alcohol.

7. Drink plenty of water, usually eight to ten glasses a day.

A couple of years ago I got an appointment with the number one cholesterol doctor in the world at Duke University Hospital in Durham, North Carolina. The first thing he said to me was, "I can see from your blood chemistry that you cannot take the cholesterol medicine that your local doctor has been prescribing. That is not a problem. We can fix just about anything with vegetables and exercise."

> *"You can fix just about anything with vegetables and exercise."*
> Mary Monroe

I think he had been talking to my Mother!

Lost in the Paris Airport

Your world will be the same tomorrow as it is today,
except for the places you go, the people you meet,
and the books you read.
Mary Monroe

The airplane was about to take off from Paris to London, but Mother's seat was empty. I was 15 years old and Mother and I were on a three-week tour of Europe. We visited Italy, Germany, Austria, Switzerland and France. It was now time to fly from Paris to London and then home, but Mother was not on the plane. I wondered if she was lost inside the airport. I was not worried because I was with the other teenagers on the tour. Well, I guess I was a little worried.

The flight attendants were making final announcements and closing up the plane when I saw Mother skid to a stop, just inside the aircraft door. She was white as a ghost and shaking like a leaf. I waved at her to get her attention and when she saw me she burst into tears, snatched me out of my seat and almost broke my neck hugging me.

"I could not find you in the airport and nobody spoke English and I was running around frantically trying to find you! Where did you go? Where did you disappear to? Why did you get on the plane with your friends without telling me? Don't you ever do that to me again! Move over and let me sit down! Don't leave my side again! Don't you ever walk away from me like that again without telling me where you are going! Don't you do that to me again, I almost died in there thinking I had lost you! Don't do that again! Why don't you answer me? You gave me a world of fright! I have never been so upset in my life! You are grounded for the next 30 years! I thought I lost you and was leaving you in the Paris Airport with people who only spoke French."

Remember those times when you had done something wrong and your parents threw so many statements and questions at you so fast, that you could not even respond? Needless to say, I stayed right beside Mother for the rest of that trip.

Before our trip to Europe, Mother told me, "If we are going to grow out of our little world on our farm in North Carolina, we will have to travel and see the world, meet new people and read more books."

Mother was right. Mother had to change her life to gain self-esteem and build financial independence for her family. Traveling, reading and meeting new people was a great way to accomplish that. *Your world will be the same tomorrow as it is today, except for the places you go, the people you meet and the books you read.*

> *Your world will be the same tomorrow as it is today, except for the places you go, the people you meet, and the books you read.*

Mother loved to travel and she took us with her to see most of the eastern United States, the Caribbean, Europe, Hawaii and the Orient. When she could not travel she would drag me along to the high school to watch travelogues. Travelogues were movies shown at the local high school made by people who traveled to exotic locations around the world. Today, you find these shows on the Travel Channel or National Geographic. Mother knew that travel is a great way to learn.

Mother believed meeting new people with different backgrounds and ideas was a great way to learn, grow and change. New people have new ideas, and getting to know them can change your outlook on life. People older than you have experiences to draw on that you don't have. Younger people have ideas and different views on life. She believed that if you surround yourself with people that share your same views, you never challenge yourself to think differently. Mother met people all over North Carolina as a way of growing and changing.

Mother read new books constantly and would read and reread a book over and over again to draw every ounce of knowledge from it. She was very selective about her reading. She would focus on one topic or author at a time.

When did you read your last book? What new things did you learn on your last trip? When was the last time you visited a museum in your home town or took a class at the community college to learn something new? When was the last time you met a new person and learned about their life?

My wife and I were just in Lynchburg, Virginia at a speaking event and we took time to visit Thomas Jefferson's home at Poplar Forest. It was the dead of winter and we took the guided tour with a father and his two school age children. I am sure the children liked being out of school and learned more about Thomas Jefferson from the tour guide than they ever would in a classroom.

Read more, travel more and meet as many new people as possible because as Mother would say, *"Your world will be the same tomorrow as it is today, except for the places you go, the people you meet, and the books you read."*

Kaboom!

"Sometimes you just have to stop and clean up your mess."
Mary Monroe

"Go get some gasoline!" Mother said emphatically.

Just before dark, the wind usually dies down as the day seems to finally rest, and that is the time that Mother choose to burn the trash pile. It wasn't really trash. Whenever we found fallen tree limbs, cuttings from a bush or trimmings from the hedges, we piled the limbs and leaves in the side pasture where the horses were and called it "the trash pile." After a month or two it had grown large enough that it needed to be burned.

Burning the pile was always fun, especially for a boy. We gathered shovels and pitchforks to help rearrange the burning limbs as they shifted and had a strong garden hose with water ready just in case the fire got out of control.

Today the trash pile was wet from a recent rain and we were having trouble lighting it. After several attempts trying to get the fire started by lighting wadded up newspaper pushed under the limbs, Mother made an executive decision...gasoline!

"Go get the gas can and let's get this fire started," she said impatiently. Well, this was going to be fun. With more than a little excitement, I retrieved the gas can, doused the pile thoroughly and was now standing back lobbing matches into the pile in hopes that one of them would stay lit long enough to ignite the gasoline and start the fire.

"What are you doing?" she demanded.

"I am trying to light the trash pile, what does it look like?"

"It looks to me like you are wasting time. Now get in there and light this fire!" And with those words ringing in my ears, I crouched down at the corner of the trash pile, retrieved another kitchen match from the box and struck the match against the starter strip on the side of the box. All I remember is seeing the match hit the starter strip and spark. KABOOM! The explosion from the gas fumes igniting blew me backwards about ten feet. I landed at Mother's feet.

The hair on my arms were all burned off. The hair on half my head was gone. My eyebrows were gone and my eyelashes were little stubbles with melted hair dots at their ends. Mother was terrified, but I was in too much shock to be afraid. We both suddenly realized

"Sometimes you just have to stop and clean up your mess."
Mary Monroe

how dangerous igniting gasoline was. She said, "Well, we have both learned something today."

I learned you should never light a gasoline fire with a match. I learned that being in an explosion is not frightening until after it is over. I think Mother learned that sometimes you have to listen to your sixteen year old son. Once the excitement of the explosion was over and the fire was merrily doing its job, consuming our trash pile, the dog and I were left with the job of supervising the fire. There was not much to do now that the excitement was over but poke the burning limbs back into the pile and think.

Burning a pile of limbs is therapeutic because it allows you to quickly clean up all the mess you have created over a long period of time. Sometimes you have to stop and clean up your mess. Life is like burning the trash pile. Every now and then, you just simply have to stop and get rid of all the things that are standing in your way, clogging up your mind and preventing you from productive work. Your outer world reflects your inner world, so start by cleaning up your outer world. When you clean up your environment, it reflects in your thinking. Burn the trash pile of your life, so to speak.

In my consulting business, I help businesses clean up their messes all the time. I have a client that is a major company in Tennessee. When I first analyzed this company, I realized that they simply had not cleaned up their company in years. It was not trash in the offices that was the problem; it was the people. This company had allowed their employees to become lazy and wasteful of their time and productive ability. All I did was teach them what Mother taught me when I was 16. It was time for this company to "burn the trash pile."

After a careful analysis, the company helped some of their employees find other places of employment, re-trained the ones who were coachable into a higher productive methodology and encouraged their top producers to accomplish more. Soon this company was running smoothly again with a highly efficient staff, but it took "burning their trash pile" to get this company moving again.

Every time I work on cleaning up my life, I think of the burning pile. Burning the pile of trash taught me how to gather my problems and clean them up. I don't mean that you should burn your problems, but every now and then you simply have to stop and clean up your own mess.

I just don't recommend you use gasoline!

Mowing the Ditch

"On the road to success, there are many
tempting parking spaces."
Today's Chuckle from the *Fayetteville Observer*
taped to my bedroom mirror by Mother

Our house sat behind a five acre pasture that was filled with red topped clover and Black Angus cows. One of my many summer jobs was to mow the grass in the ditch that separated that pasture from Middle Road. It was a long ditch. It was a very, very, very long ditch. It became longer when you had to cut it every week with a push mower in the hot North Carolina sun. Mowing that ditch was not fun, but someone had to do it, and that someone, according to Mother, was me. Mother would say, "Son, I can't help you with this. It's got to be done and you're the only one who can do it."

The easy part was cutting the grass on both sides of the ditch with the riding lawn mower. Then I had to clean the pinecones, trash and bottles out of the bottom of the ditch before I could mow the ditch itself. The entire job took half a day.

At some point while mowing that ditch, I always wanted to quit. Aunt Margaret ran a bake shop in the back of her house on the other side of Middle Road. She started her bake shop to create income for her family after her husband died suddenly. If the wind was blowing from the south, it would bring the smell of freshly baked cakes, pies and cookies from Margaret's Bake Shop. That smell would make it almost impossible to cut the grass in the

24

ditch without giving into my hunger by crossing the road and helping myself to whatever goodies Aunt Margaret would share.

Mother would not allow me to return to the house until the job was done, unless one of the mowers broke down or ran out of gas. It would be difficult to explain to Mother why I stopped cutting the ditch and walked over to Aunt Margaret's to ask her for a piece of her famous pound cake or a snicker-doodle cookie. Cutting that ditch taught me to resist the temptation to quit once I started something. I stuck it out and finished because Mother was counting on me. Cutting that ditch taught me to work against the greatest obstacle in life...myself.

Mother would say, *"On the road to success, there are many tempting parking spaces."*

Mother could not quit in her efforts to run the farm, learn about business and discover the philosophy that would enable her to be successful. I could not quit because Mother depended on me to help her on her journey. Later in life, when things got tough, I would remember mowing that ditch and know that if I could finish the job with the smell of cakes and pies in the air, I could accomplish anything. *Everything you accomplish in life prepares you to accomplish something else.* When you start something that you have done before, you know that you can finish it, and as you complete more and more tasks, your sense of accomplishment grows. It takes a while, but eventually you realize that anything is possible, as long as you don't quit.

Cutting the ditch was not the only thing I did as a young boy.

I also played tennis. My father was an avid tennis player and he built a tennis court on our farm when I was six years old. I played tennis with friends and family until I got to high school where I discovered I was a pretty good tennis player.

My freshman year of college I attended a school in Florida and played tennis for them. My sophomore year I transferred to N.C. State University with the hope of playing tennis in the Atlantic Coast Conference. There was only one scholarship for tennis at N.C. State University and John Sadri had it. I was an unknown player without a national ranking so I had to try out for the team.

The first day of tryouts there were ninety players trying out for two spots on the team! All ninety of us practiced on eight clay tennis courts at the same time. It was crowded. We hit tennis balls in between the courts, in the corners, and anywhere we could find an open space. Coach Isenhour watched us play and at the end of the first day he told fifteen or twenty players not to come back. Every day we played, the coach watched, and fifteen or twenty players were asked not to come back the next day. Practice was so difficult and physically demanding that a lot of them just quit and never came back.

At the end of the two weeks of practice I had lost fifteen pounds and there were only two players left, Jere Booke from Pennsylvania, and myself. We were the only two to make the North Carolina State University Tennis Team out of ninety players! People were amazed that I had not quit in the two weeks of grueling workouts. Obviously, they never watched me mow the ditch!

More than once, when I finished cutting the ditch, and took a moment to admire my completed work, I would hear a, "Yoo-hoo!" from across the road. Aunt Margaret would be in her front yard waving for me to come over. She would say, "I just baked a wedding cake and had to cut the crust off the top to make it stack properly. Would you like to take some of these cake shavings to your mother?"

Aunt Margaret's wedding cakes were pure butter pound cakes, and everyone knows the best part of a pound cake is the top half inch of crust. Aunt Margaret had cut the crust off the pound cake and put it in a bread sack and was offering it to me (and she had to ask if I wanted it).

> *"On the road to success, there are many tempting parking spaces."*
> *Today's Chuckle* from the *Fayetteville Observer* taped to my bedroom mirror by Mother

We have all had to learn how to delay rewards or gratification until the job is finished. Nothing is better than rewarding yourself after accomplishing a difficult task. There is certainly nothing better than spending a summer day cutting a ditch with a push lawnmower and having Mother toast a piece of Aunt Margaret's pound cake and put ice cream on it as a treat.

When was the last time you refused to quit? When was the last time you pushed through adversity to succeed? When was the last time you treated yourself to a piece of toasted pound cake?

You can accomplish anything if you don't quit. Remember Mother's lesson: *On the road to success, there are many tempting parking spaces.*

Plateau Learning

"Nothing happens overnight, but when it happens,
it happens overnight!"
Phil Bellamy

In late February, when the sky is gray and the wind is cold, Mother would walk her yard and plan for the spring. If you walked with her, she would show you the hidden growth in the plants and trees. The trees would already have buds and the daffodils would be pushing through the warming earth, which you might miss if Mother did not know show it to you.

Everything has a growing season. Plants appear to sit idle all winter, but they are really storing energy in their roots and trunk in preparation for spring. When spring arrives, there is an explosion of growth. Nothing happens overnight, but when it happens, it happens overnight! The rapid growth of spring is replaced with maturing as summer arrives. In late summer, a plant's energy is directed toward storing food and in the fall, the trees and plants begin to lose their leaves. During winter, the plants seem to sit idle and the cycle begins again.

A plant's growth follows the change in the seasons, which we consider normal. When you study nature, you realize that everything follows the same pattern of storing energy, rapid growth, maturity and resting, while storing energy for the next growth season.

People are a lot like plants. We learn and store knowledge

without any visible sign of advancement. Then, just like plants in the spring, we grow rapidly to a new plateau where we level off and learn again before the cycle repeats itself. Most growth occurs on the plateau with no outward visible signs.

As a U.S.P.T.A. Tennis Professional, I found that tennis players do not advance their tennis skills on a gradual incline. Instead, they advance in steps or platforms. A new player has to practice hitting a tennis ball again and again until it becomes muscle memory. After days or weeks of practice, suddenly one day they can hit the shot they always wanted. A tennis player must spend hundreds of hours practicing to reach the next plateau.

Nothing happens overnight, but when it happens, it happens overnight!

I call this growth cycle *plateau learning.* There are four distinct steps to plateau learning.

1. We store knowledge and information through study and practice.
2. We mature and internalize a skill or knowledge.
3. Rapid growth and advancement. *The advancements seem to happen overnight.*
4. Rest and celebrate while enjoying our accomplishments, which starts the cycle all over again.

Most of your work at a new skill occurs on the plateau without any visible results. Then suddenly, one day you reach a new level, a new plateau of performance. That spurt upward marks the moment when the results of your hard work and study finally took effect. The upward spurts vary, and the plateau has its own dips and rises, but after a spurt of advancement you will reach a higher plateau where your next level of learning begins.

Practice diligently to hone your skills to attain a new level of competence, and be willing to spend most of your time on the plateau without visible results. Keep studying and practicing even when you seem to be getting nowhere. You must put in the hours of practice and study until you take another quantum leap and reach a new plateau.

Karl Pribram, professor of neuroscience at Stanford University, calls it a "habitual behavior system." This habit system involves the reflex circuits in the spinal cord as well as in various parts of the brain to which it is connected. This habitual system makes it possible to do things, like hit a tennis ball without consciously having to think about it.

Thinking is part of the cognitive system of your brain. When you learn a new skill you have to think about how to do it. You form a new habit by replacing old patterns of thought with new patterns. You move to a new plateau when you can do something without thinking about it. You have formed a new habit.

To master anything takes time. To learn a sport or become financially independent takes time. There is no quick fix. There is no quick way to riches. Everyone who becomes a master at anything took time in diligent, high quality, long-term practice and study.

Today, our culture bombards us with promises of fast, easy results and instant gratification. We are promised maximum results with minimum practice; instant enlightenment, overnight learning and total fitness in 30 minutes a week. No need to practice. No need to study. No need to spend time learning. We are promised instant knowledge, cosmic enlightenment and a universal mind that will allow us to know all things without having to put forth any effort.

Mother would tell you that is "bunk." You must study, practice and think deeply to become knowledgeable in any subject. While talent is important, practice is a far more important factor in high level performance.

> *"Nothing happens overnight, but when it happens, it happens overnight!"*
> Phil Bellamy

Research shows it takes ten thousand hours of practice to be a master at your chosen field of endeavor.

Mother started life with self-doubts and easily could have been broken, but she grew from plateau to plateau until she was a strong, self-confident woman.

Are you willing to work hard enough to move to the next plateau? Will you develop the skills necessary to make your life a success?

Remember, *nothing happens overnight, but when it happens, it happens overnight!"*

LESSON 2

A Man's Mind
is Like a Garden

*Mary Monroe and her granddaughter,
Louisa Monroe, playing in the dirt*

Philosophy: Who Needs It?

*"The question 'to be or not to be' is the question
'to think or not to think.'"*
From Ayn Rand's West Point graduation address titled,
Philosophy: Who Needs It?

Mother was excited to find an oriental tapestry rug with frayed edges on one of her shopping trips to an antique store. When she brought it home, she made me move all the furniture in the living room out of the way, and then carry that heavy, dusty old rug in from the car and put it on the floor in just the right spot. Mother stood back and admired her purchase. It just looked like an old rug to me.

Mother told me to observe the image woven into that tapestry rug. It had beautiful colors that created a wonderful pattern. Each thread was a slightly different color, and when they all came together, they created an image with a magnificent blend of colors. Maybe there was more to that old rug than I first thought.

A tapestry is an image created in fabric, which is built by weaving many different colored threads together. Your mind works exactly the same way as an artist weaving a tapestry. Tapestry thinking is when you weave many different thoughts together to create knowledge or beliefs. Mother taught us that thinking deeply was important. You simply gather the threads of information into knowledge to help you reach a philosophy for your life.

Mother had been taught since childhood that all she had to do was follow the advice of her parents, husband, church or govern-ment and her life would work out just fine. When her husband died she realized that she had to think for herself. A philosophy is a system of how to think. It is the sum total of your thoughts and beliefs. Here is what Ayn Rand said about philosophy in her West Point Commencement address titled, *Philosophy: Who Needs It?*

"A Philosophic system is an integrated view of existence. As a human being, you have no choice about the fact that you need a philosophy. Your only choice is whether you define your phi-losophy by a conscious, rational, disciplined process of thought and scrupulously logical deliberation – or let your subconscious accumulate a junk heap of unwarranted conclusions, false gen-eralizations, (and) undefined contractions."

We all have a philosophy that runs our life; we have no choice in the matter. We do however, have a choice in what philosophy we adopt. Your philosophy integrates your observations, experi-ences and knowledge into abstract ideas and principles that help you deal with concrete, particular, real-life problems. Each of us has the awesome responsibility to manage and control our own thoughts and form our own philosophy.

A newborn child starts life without a philosophy. Each new ob-ject is a unique phenomenon to a baby, but as the child grows they begin to learn the blob that enters its awareness is its mother. Later it learns that its mother is the source of food, and, still later, the child learns that its mother has a name, feelings and individual character.

This path of discovery is the same path that each of us had to take in order to learn to think. We must make exacting, rational and disciplined choices about what information we accept as truth to build our philosophy. Forming a philosophy requires rational thought. It requires us to think.

Ayn Rand continues, *"THE APHORISM, 'As a man thinketh in his heart so is he,' not only embraces the whole of a man's being, but is so comprehensive as to reach out to every condition and circumstance of his life. A man is literally what he thinks, his character being the complete sum of all his thoughts."*

You cannot accept ideas at random and count them as knowledge merely because you feel like it. You must learn how to use your mind, how to distinguish truth from falsehood and how to validate the conclusions you reach. There can be no conflict between what you know

"The question 'to be or not to be' is the question 'to think or not to think.'"
From Ayn Rand's West Point graduation address, titled: *Philosophy: Who Needs It?*

and how you know it. When you align your knowledge and beliefs with your actions, you reach a state of philosophic integrity. To think is an act of choice. Reason does not work automatically.

Ayn Rand continues, *"Thinking is not a mechanical process; the connections of logic are not made by instinct. The function of your stomach, lungs, or heart is automatic; the function of your mind is not. In any hour and issue of your life, you are free to think or to evade that effort. But you are not free to escape from your nature, from the fact that reason is your means of survival – so that for you, who are a human being, the question 'to be or not to be' is the question 'to think or not to think.'"*

A philosophy is a system of how to think, and your mind is like a tapestry rug. You must weave many different thoughts together to create *your own* philosophy of life. It is easy to adopt the beliefs, religion or political party of your family or community because that is how you were raised. But thinking is hard work. It is difficult to think for yourself and create your own philosophy of life, but your philosophy enables you to deal with the real life problems we face every day. Just remember that the question "to be or not to be" is the question "to think or not to think."

A Man's Mind is Like a Garden

*"Dirt doesn't care what you plant in it;
neither does your mind."*
Mary Monroe

Mother was a master gardener. If you ever wanted to find her, all you had to do was look in the yard. She was always planting, pruning, digging, chopping or pulling weeds. Mother was also the master gardener of her life. She tended her mind like she tended her garden. She was very careful to cultivate the thoughts and beliefs that she wanted to grow there. She was just as careful to pull any negative or limiting beliefs from her mind, just as she would pull weeds from her garden.

If you were talking to Mother in the yard, she would unconsciously kneel down to pull a few weeds while you were in conversation. She would say, *"Dirt doesn't care what you plant in it; neither does your mind."* To make your garden grow, you have to plant the right seeds in the right place at the right time. Your mind is just like your garden. It doesn't care what kind of thoughts and beliefs you plant in it. Positive or negative thoughts will grow equally well.

One of the books Mother read was *As a Man Thinketh*, written in 1902, by James Allen. He was a businessman who at the age of 27, decided to retire and become a writer. Here is what James Allan had to say about planting the right thoughts in your mind: *"A man's mind may be likened to a garden, which may be intelligently cultivated or allowed to run wild; but whether cultivated or neglected, it must, and will, bring forth. If no useful seeds are put into it, then an abundance of useless weed-seeds will fall therein, and will continue to produce their kind.*

"Just as a gardener cultivates his plot, keeping it free from weeds, and growing the flowers and fruits which he requires, so may a man tend the garden of his mind, weeding out all the wrong, useless, and impure thoughts, and cultivating toward perfection the flowers and fruits of right, useful, and pure thoughts. By pursuing this process, a man sooner or later discovers that he is the master gardener of his soul, the director of his life."

Without self-discipline in your thinking, you become like a garden taken over by weeds. You are the only person responsible for disciplining your mind. You are the only person responsible for how you think.

James Allen continues, *"Thought and character are one, and as character can only manifest and discover itself through environment and circumstance, the outer conditions of a person's life will always be found to be harmoniously related to his inner state."*

Your thoughts become your beliefs and your beliefs guide your actions. Your actions create your character. Your character becomes a reflection of your thoughts and beliefs. If you want to change your life, you must first change your thoughts.

Mother lived every day in harmony with the reality of the world around her because her values and actions were aligned.

She always looked within herself to find the answer to any problem because she was the master gardener of her own life.

You cannot have in your life that which you are not. If you want love in your life, are you a loving person? If you want wealth in your life, do you respect money? If you want success in your life, do you live with self-discipline? You cannot have love in your life, if you do not love. You cannot have wealth if you spend all your money. You cannot be successful, without disciplining your actions. It is up to you and no one else. You created the life you are currently living by the choices

"Dirt doesn't care what you plant in it; neither does your mind."
Mary Monroe

you have made and if you are not happy with your life today, you simply have to make new choices.

When you align your actions with your values, you will have planted the seeds of integrity in your life. Take the time to clearly define what your beliefs are, and then determine if your actions are aligned with those beliefs. If you are willing to do the difficult work of self-examination you will discover that you can change your life by changing your philosophy.

James Allen continues, *"Good thoughts and actions can never produce bad results; bad thoughts and actions can never produce good results."*

Mother taught that your mind is like your garden. Weeds in the garden choke the sunlight from your plants, and the weeds in your mind can choke out good thoughts. Weeds in your mind are all those negative and limiting thoughts that choke the positive beliefs from your life. Weeds grow in your mind all the time and you don't even notice them. You must weed your mind a little bit every day.

Where I live the trash man comes on Thursday mornings. I had just taken the trash to the cur, when on the way back to the house, I stopped to pull a weed from the monkey grass planted between the driveway and the side walk. Then I noticed another weed, so I pulled it out, and then another, and anotherand another. I thought there was only one weed when I started, but after a few minutes I realized that the monkey grass was full of weeds. Weeds were everywhere. All kinds of weeds! There were broad leaf weeds, clover and crab grass. There were so many weeds that it was hard to tell the difference between what we had planted and what had sprung up uninvited. I spent the next five minutes weeding the monkey grass, and when I stopped to see what I had accomplished, I realized that I had made quite a difference in how the bed looked.

Step back and observe your life, and appreciate it for the joy it brings. Today, become the master gardener of your life. Take the time to weed your mind, removing all the negative thoughts or beliefs that are growing there, and plant positive, uplifting and inspirational thoughts. Before you go charging out into the world today, stop and take a moment to enjoy your own life like you enjoy your garden. Appreciate the beauty of your mind and the life you have created. You are giving your mind a dose of "fertilizer."

Stop and give thanks for the garden you call your mind, and remember what Mother would say, *"Dirt doesn't care what you plant in it; neither does your mind."*

Root Bound

"Your thoughts create your beliefs.
Your beliefs control your actions.
Your actions determine your results."
Zan Monroe

Mama said, "Today we were going to repot plants."

She had started the tiny plants in little pots, and now they had grown too big for their containers. She showed me how to remove the plants from their pots and transfer them to the new larger containers. Mother would take the plant out of its container, and gently break the roots apart before replanting it. She broke up the roots so the plant could get water and nutrients without having to transport them so far. After the plant was repotted, it would not grow for a while until the roots re-established themselves in a new environment. Then it would grow within the expanded limits of its new home. When a plant had no more room to grow Mother called it "root bound."

"You have to be gentle with their roots because moving them is traumatic and will hurt a little," Mother would say.

"If it hurts, can I hear the plants scream?" I asked. A fifteen year old boy wants to hear plants scream. I was disappointed that I never heard a plant scream.

People become root bound, too. You have a pot that creates the boundaries of your life. Your pot is your limiting beliefs that create the size of your world. When you stop growing and learning, you become root bound. You hold yourself back by your belief of what you can and cannot do. You prevent yourself from achieving more in life because you become comfortable in your own little container. The amount of money you earn, the job you have, who you love, how big your life is are all controlled by the size of your belief system. When you experience new things, read, travel or meet new people you, expand your perceptual map.

You are the only person who is capable of setting limits on your growth. Only you can change yourself, expand your beliefs and get yourself growing again. Your life does not change when your boss changes, when your friends change, when your parents change, when your spouse changes or when your company changes. Your life changes when you change your beliefs. Your life will change when you go beyond your limiting beliefs, when you realize that *you* are the only one responsible for your life and finally take charge of that responsibility.

One of Mother's favorite stories was about the fisherman who kept all the small fish and threw back the big ones. When his friend asked why he threw the bigger fish back he replied, "Because I have a nine inch frying pan and I can only keep the fish that will fit into it."

"Why don't you get a bigger frying pan?" his friend asked.

"Oh no, I could never do that. I come from a long line of nine-inch frying pan people. My daddy had a nine-inch frying pan. My grandpa had a nine-inch frying pan. We are just nine inch frying pan people."

Anything is possible in your life, but first you must change yourself into a new, rich environment where you will not be root bound and you can grow again. It is time to break out of your self-imposed prison and repot yourself into a larger life. You must find a larger container for your life.

"Your thoughts create your beliefs. Your beliefs control your actions Your actions determine your results."
Zan Monroe

Push your limits. Try a new recipe, take a class, and attempt something new. Just try! Your relationships, your business, your finances, your educational and spiritual growth are all limited by your beliefs. You have become root bound because of your thinking.

Remember, *"Your thoughts create your beliefs. Your beliefs control your actions. Your actions determine your results."*

Reason, Purpose and Self-Esteem

"Being in charge of your own life
is your highest personal responsibility"
Mary Monroe

Mother was a young girl in the early 1900's when women did not have the right to vote. She grew up with her parents saying she should be "seen and not heard," and that girls could not do things because they were girls. The church told her that she was a worthless sinner. Higher educational opportunities were not available. Society was telling her that the only work a woman could expect was that of a secretary, nurse, teacher or housewife. A woman's job was to support her husband and raise their children.

Mother accepted this role in society until her husband died suddenly in 1965. Then she broke out of a lifetime of self-doubt and low self-esteem created by the society and culture she lived in, to become a powerful self-made woman.

A mother's love is a powerful force, and it drove Mother to do things that women of the 1960's and 70's simply were not expected or allowed to do. With very little formal education, but a great yearn for learning and taking action, she started businesses, built houses and worked in political parties which were all male dominated fields. Mother forged ahead because she knew that she had to become a woman of self-esteem and financial independence in order to set an example for her children.

Mother found a voice of reason in philosopher and novelist Ayn Rand, who helped forge Mother's new philosophy of life. Ayn Rand's books and teachings resonated within Mother as the truth and were incorporated into her new belief system. Here is a powerful statement that helped Mother in her journey to success from Ayn Rand's novel, *Atlas Shrugged:*

To live, man must hold three things as the supreme and ruling values of his life; Reason – Purpose – Self-esteem. Reason, as his only tool of knowledge; Purpose, as his choice of the happiness which that tool must proceed to achieve; Self-esteem as his inviolate certainty that his mind is competent to think and his person is worthy of happiness, which means; is worthy of living.

Mother taught us that *reason* is your ability to think, to manage your thoughts and to reach the logical decisions that further your life. Your mind is your only tool of survival. The human animal doesn't have long teeth, sharp claws or thick fur like other animals. Our only tool of survival is our ability to think, reason, and to take seemingly unrelated information and assimilate it into knowledge. Successful people make decisions and take action based on that knowledge.

Purpose is the guiding principal of every person's life. All human activity is purpose-directed. Without purpose, life has no meaning. To be truly alive, you have to have a clearly defined purpose for your life.

Self-esteem is the belief that you are worthy of a life of happiness, that you are competent to think, make your own decisions,

48

and be worthy of living the life that you have chosen. It is your unshakable belief in yourself and an unwavering personal honesty with yourself and the rest of the world.

Mother always said, *"Being in charge of your own life is your highest personal responsibility."*

Mother would meet problems head on, without delay, and make decisions based on her own judgment. She would say, "When you encounter a problem, immediately look for answers and make a decision. Don't tread water over a problem but decide and move forward. If you discover later you have made the wrong decision, you can always fix it by making a new decision."

> *"Being in charge of your own life is your highest personal responsibility"*
> Mary Monroe

She learned to live her life and forget what the rest of the world thought. She would not alter the truth in any way to accommodate the wishes of others.

Let your journey in life be guided by this statement, *"To live, a man must hold three things as supreme and ruling values of his life: reason, purpose and self-esteem."*

I Do Not Choose To Be A Common Man

My Creed, By Dean Alfange

For my 14th birthday, Mother gave me a framed copper etching titled, My Creed, by Dean Alfange. I would have preferred a new tennis racket or some basketball shoes, but it was a gift from Mother so it was fine.

She hung the etching on the wall at the foot of my bed and every night I saw the framed words staring back at me, and every morning they greeted me with the sunrise. As time went by, I realized that I was reading the plaque every day without knowing it and the words were having an effect on me.

Here is what was etched on that copper plate.

My Creed, by Dean Alfange

I do not choose to be a common man.

It is my right to be uncommon – if I can. I seek opportunity – not security.

I do not wish to be a kept citizen, humbled and dulled by having the state look after me.

I want to take the calculated risk; to dream and to build, to fail and to succeed.

I refuse to barter incentive for a dole. I prefer the challenges of life to the guaranteed existence; the thrill of fulfillment to the stale calm of utopia.

I will not trade freedom for beneficence, nor my dignity for a handout. I will never cower before any master nor bend to any threat.

It is my heritage to stand erect, proud and unafraid; to think and act for myself, enjoy the benefit of my creations and to face the world boldly and say, This I have done.

All this is what it means to be an American.

This plaque taught me how to live with integrity. Integrity is defined as (1) A firm adherence to a code of moral or artistic values; Incorruptibility (2) An unimpaired condition of soundness; (3) The quality or state of being complete or undivided.

Integrity is wholeness or completeness. The surface of a balloon has integrity because if there's a flaw anywhere, the balloon pops. Your life is just like a balloon; a complete and total entity.

If you choose to live a life of integrity, your values and actions must be aligned. Your life is balanced in thought and deed. A life that is lived with integrity does not fight against itself. Without resistance, there is no strain to living. You live at peace with yourself and everything you do. You are following your dreams. Such a life has within it all the seeds of success. Those parts all complement each other to nurture a life of completeness and peace which is most important to you.

In my work, with some of the world's most successful companies, I have discovered they all have something in common. Successful companies, like successful people, follow a clearly defined creed or code of behavior. My clients who excel, state their creed or code of behavior for the world to see. This statement establishes the standards, philosophy and core values of their organization.

It becomes an affirmation for the entire company to internalize. That affirmation changes the way the employees think, which changes their belief system, which changes their actions and production. If you want to make your organization function better and raise production, create a creed for everyone to follow.

Over time, Dean Alfange's creed became my own, and now I live by it every day. Today, the Dean Alfange copper etching hangs in my son's room. I hope it will become his creed, too. It will help him understand what it means to live a life of integrity. I hope he chooses not to be a common man.

Do you have a personal creed or philosophy? Can you write it out and define it? Is it hanging on the wall in your office or home? If you don't, you can always borrow mine.

Cutting Down the Sweet Gum Tree

"Focus is the key to success, not force."
Mary Monroe

It was a crisp, cool, fall day in North Carolina; just perfect to play football with my cousins, but that was not my fate for this day. Today, I was working for Mother. Today was the day that she wanted me to cut down a sweet gum tree on the ditch bank behind the house.

I gathered my gloves and ax, and trudged out in the yard to begin the daunting task of cutting down a tree by hand. No chain saw; just me, an ax and the tree. I felt a sense of awe knowing that for thousands of years men had cut down trees this way.

Swinging an ax will quickly put muscles on a young man. As a fourteen year old boy I was fast becoming a man. Mostly bone and muscle, I had developed quickly and with the supervision of Mother and with the help of this tree, I was about to develop some more.

After sharpening the ax and clearing the small underbrush from the base of the tree, I was ready to begin. The first strike of an ax into a tree trunk is satisfying. The ax bites deep into the bark and makes you think you are getting somewhere fast. You think, "This is going to be easy. It will not take me any time to cut this tree down." You better think again!

It did not take long for me to break the bark off the tree and discover that the tree was going to put up a struggle. Under the soft bark is the tough trunk of the tree, where the wood is much dense and I discovered quickly that just hitting the tree with the ax would not make the tree fall over. Another plan was called for.

About that time Mother came by. She always seemed to know just when a young man needed a break and some encouragement.

"I used to watch my daddy swing an ax and it always seemed to me that he never swung very hard, but the ax always landed in the exact spot he wanted it to. And when the ax landed in the right spot, the wood chips just flew out of the tree. My father told me once that he was just like the sculptor who said that the statue is held captive within the rock, and all he had to do is remove everything else. Well, cutting down a tree would be the same thing. There are chips inside the tree that must come out to make the tree fall. Your job is to remove those chips like a sculptor. The key to your success is your ability to focus on where the ax will land. If it hits the right spot, the chips will fly. It does not make any difference how hard you swing. It matters where the ax lands. *Focus is the key to success, not force.*"

And then she moved off to do something else in the yard, while I was left under the supervision of the dog. *"Focus was the key to success, not force,"* she said. I focused on the precise spot in the tree, the ax fell exactly where I wanted it to, and a chip flew out of the tree. Another swing and another wood chip was gone. *"Just like a sculptor,"* I thought. Focus was the key to success, not force. Focus and effort. Effort and focus. This stuff really works!

There is something therapeutic about working with your

muscles; it gives you time to think. And while the ax swung and the chips flew, I began to realize that Mother was right, focus is the key to success.

Life is like cutting down a tree with an ax. Focus is the key, not force. I have learned that there are three steps that will help you focus your world.

Step one is making a plan, gathering your tools, sharpening your skills and getting your gloves to protect against life's blisters.

"Focus is the key to success, not force."
Mary Monroe

Step two is remembering that *focus is the key to success, not force.* Focus on what you want. Focus on hitting the right spots in life and not brute force. Focus on getting the best out of every moment and every activity. The great artists, business people and athletes all have the ability to focus and block out everything else.

Step three is staying with your goal until you have achieved it. Most people never focus on one thing long enough to make a difference in their life. They never stay focused on a dream or a vision or a goal long enough to see the chips fly. They only beat the bark off their dreams, and then when the going gets tough, they stop focusing and give up. When their focus is gone, they try brute force to make things happen, and that never produces the results they want.

Life is just like cutting down a tree with an ax. *Focus is the key to success, not force.*

While I was focused on making the chips fly, I lost track of time, and before I knew it, the tree began to creak and moan, and then with a snap, it collapsed into the yard. Mother reappeared and said, "Nice job. Now, as soon as you remove all the limbs, haul them to the burning pile and cut the trunk into small enough pieces to burn in the fireplace, you can go play football with your cousins."

There would be no football for me today. Finishing off the tree would take the rest of the day. Football did not matter any longer because Mother's task had taught her lesson. Focus on accomplishing your goals and remove all obstacles one by one like removing wood chips from a tree, and you can achieve anything.

Life is like cutting down a tree with an ax. *Focus is the key to success, not force.*

LESSON 3

Do What You Enjoy;
You Will Be Good at It

Mary Monroe in her garden
1990

Downy Duck Learns to Fly

"Talent does what it can, but genius does what it must!"
Mary Monroe

Downy Duck Grows Up was a children's book that Mother read to me when I was young. One of my favorite stories was *Downy Duck Learns to Fly.* It went something like this:

One day Downy Duck's mother said to all her little ducklings, "Today we are going to learn to fly."

Downy Duck replied, "I don't want to learn to fly. I want to climb a tree, so I can sit on a limb and see the entire world!"

His mother said, "Ducks cannot climb trees. A Duck is made to swim and fly, and today is the day for you to learn to fly."

"Well, today I want to learn to climb a tree," said Downy Duck, and he set off into the forest to do just that.

Downy Duck came upon a squirrel and asked, "Can you teach me to climb a tree?"

"No," replied the squirrel, "you don't have claws to climb with. Why don't you learn to fly like all the other ducks?"

Downy Duck asked the cat, "Can you teach me how to climb a tree?"

"No," replied the cat, "you don't have claws to climb with. Why don't you learn to fly like all the other ducks?"

Downy Duck went all over the forest trying to find somebody to help him climb a tree so he could sit on a limb and see the great big world, but he could not find anyone that would help him.

Downy Duck was very sad as he walked home through the forest. Then he heard his mother calling to him from overhead. Looking up he discovered his mother and all his brothers and sisters sitting on the limb of a tree."

"How did you climb that tree?" asked Downy Duck

"We didn't climb," replied his mother, "We flew up here, and if you had learned to fly, which is what you were born to do, you would be able to sit on a limb in this tree with us and see the entire world!"

Downy Duck finally fulfilled his dream of sitting on a limb in a tree to see the world by following his natural genius of flying. Everyone has a genius. Your job in life is to discover yours. If we apply our natural genius to our goals and dreams, we can achieve them. *Discovering your true genius should be your goal in life. Using that genius to achieve your goals should be your purpose in life.*

In his landmark book, *Frames of Mind; The Theory of Multiple Intelligences,* published in 1983, Harvard University education professor Howard Gardner unveiled a theory of multiple intelligences that rejected the traditional and long-held view that

60

aptitude consists solely of the ability to reason and understand complex ideas. You will enjoy finding your genius among the following nine types of intelligence.

1. **Naturalist Intelligence** is the ability to discriminate among living things (plants, animals) as well as sensitivity to other features of the natural world (clouds, rock formations, etc.).

2. **Musical Intelligence** is the capacity to discern pitch, rhythm, timbre and tone.

"Talent does what it can. Genius does what it must!" Mary Monroe

3. **Logical-Mathematical Intelligence** is the ability to calculate, quantify, consider propositions and hypotheses, and carry out complete mathematical operations.

4. *Existential Intelligence* is the ability to tackle deep questions about human existence, such as the meaning of life, why we die, and how did we get here.

5. **Interpersonal Intelligence** is the ability to understand and interact effectively with others.

6. **Bodily-Kinesthetic Intelligence** is the capacity to manipulate your body in a variety of physical skills.

7. **Linguistic Intelligence** is the ability to think in words and to use language to express and appreciate complex meanings. Linguistic intelligence is the most widely shared human competence and is evident in poets, novelists, journalists and effective public

speakers.

8. **Intra-personal Intelligence** is the capacity to understand your thoughts and feelings, and to use such knowledge in planning and setting a direction in your life.

9. **Spatial Intelligence** is the ability to think and manipulate objects in three dimensions.

Each person has the ability to become competent in any of these intelligence types, but you will excel at the ones where your genius lies. Each one of us has one or more type of genius from the nine listed above. Just like a duck has the genius to swim and fly, you have to follow your genius to become a success. When you discover the types of intelligence you have, you will be well on your way to finding your genius.

Remember that *talent does what it can, but genius does what it must.* Mother was talented, like we all are, but she used her genius to excel in certain areas. She used her Naturalist Intelligence to grow plants, landscape yards and turned that into a money-making business. Her Musical Intelligence was satisfied by singing in the church choir and on the radio. Her Spatial Intelligence showed itself in her ability to landscape yards and rebuild houses.

When I was in college, Mother insisted I take a landscape architecture course because she wanted me to start a landscape and lawn care business. She saw the potential for a landscape business to be very profitable. She recognized that many people would gladly pay someone who possessed the Naturalist Intelligence to take care of their yards. The problem is, I do not possess the Naturalist Intelligence. I have a digging and planting *talent* because Mother taught me how, but I lack the *genius* required to be a success in the landscaping business. I had to follow my genius of teaching, writing and inspiring others.

Follow your own genius. Don't try to become what your parents, teachers or spouse wants you to be. Take a moment to go back through the nine types of intelligence and check off the ones that you possess. If you are unsure if you have a particular type of intelligence, ask a friend or family member.

Money flows to those who find their creative genius and apply that genius to productive work. Try different things, find new friends with different talents or interests, and see what you can learn from them. They might help you discover your genius. Everything and everyone you need to succeed is right around you. Finding your intelligent genius will give you the opportunity to do something you love and make money at it. Spend time studying what other people need and apply your creative genius to that need. Highly productive people have found a way to align their creative genius with their work. Once you do that, then success flows to you.

Remember, *"Talent does what it can, but genius does what it must."*

Do What You Enjoy; You Will Be Good at It.

"Do what you enjoy, you will be good at it."
Mary Monroe

When I was a senior in high school trying to decide about my future, Mother said, "Son, do what you enjoy; you will be good at it!" I have followed that advice the rest of my life.

I have always been fascinated by water. My father taught me to swim at an early age on visits to White Lake. In Junior High School, I loved to watch The Underwater World of Jacques Cousteau as he explored the ocean. By the age of sixteen, I owned my own scuba equipment and would go scuba diving every chance I got. I read all of Jacque Cousteau's books and the U.S. Navy Diver's Manual. Two of my sisters were elementary school teachers, and I would take my scuba gear to their classrooms to explain to their students the underwater world I had discovered. It was a great way for me to get out of class and it started my career as a speaker and teacher.

I enjoyed water so much, I majored in marine biology in college, focused mainly on sharks, but found that organic chemistry and I did not get along very well. I learned that what I really enjoyed was learning about the ocean and then teaching what I knew to someone else, like I had done for my sister's elementary classes. I discovered that I was a teacher, not a scientist. I realized that my purpose in life is to create an environment where others can learn. I enjoyed teaching so much I became a speaker, writer, and consultant.

Mother always paraphrased the famous comedian Red Skelton by saying, "Find that thing you would do for free, get someone to pay you to do it, and you will have found your calling in life."

Take a moment and ask yourself, what do you spend your free time doing? What fascinates you? What are you passionate about? What do you really enjoy? What is it that you would do for free if you could? Find those things you enjoy and you will have found a vocation, not just a job.

A good friend of mine is Dave Evans. He is a business owner who has a great business marketing houses for builders and developers. I had lunch with him recently and he said, *"Put your passion into your business plan."* He is passionate about wine and has incorporated his passion into his business plan. Instead of holding open houses, Dave hosts wine tasting events in new home neighborhoods attracting REALTORS® and the general public. He sends an informative post card about wine to his clients every month.

> *"Put your passion into your business plan."*
> *David Evans*

Finding what you enjoy is easy. The key to success is figuring out how to make a living doing it. Now, if you are passionate about sitting on the couch, watching TV and eating frozen pizza, I cannot help you. I am talking about productive work, not loafing.

In the free enterprise system, an idea can make you a fortune. As my Uncle Adrian used to say, "You can make money at any thing. You just have to figure out how." Find those things in your life that you enjoy and do them to your fullest. Don't hold back. Go one hundred percent toward what you enjoy, and don't let anything stand in your way.

Can you start a business doing something you enjoy? If you did, I bet you would be good at it. *Do what you enjoy; you will be good at it* sounds so simple, you might just miss how powerful that statement really is.

I Don't Want to Go to School

"Your purpose in life is to be creative."
Mary Monroe

"I don't want to go to school today," I whined from under the covers.

Mother snatched open the blue and white striped drapes in my bedroom and said, "You have to go to school today."

"I don't feel like school. I am tired of school, and I don't want to go. I want to stay home."

My Mother then answered back with this story:

One day a boy woke up and said to his mother, "I don't want to go to school today."

"Why not?" his mother asked.

"Because, all the students hate me. All the teachers hate me. Even the lunch ladies and the custodian hate me. Everyone in that school hates me, and I just do not want to go to school today!"

His mother answered, "Well you have to go to school today because you are the Principal!"

I was always surprised when Mother told a joke. I never

thought of her as funny, but she loved a great story. Mother always had a way of teaching a lesson with a story or joke.

There were plenty of days that I simply did not want to go to school. Mother would often tell me that story, and then she would give me a choice.

"You can go to school or you can stay home and work for me!" Her eyes would always sparkle when she said it.

If you were going to skip school and stay home, Mother had you up at the crack of dawn. She was famous for having a list of work to do, and if she had me for a full day she would keep me busy working in her garden, burning trash, cutting, mowing, clipping and chopping. She knew that if I was not in school, she could work me like a dog. So I was faced with a choice; go to school, or work for Mother.

Some days it was worth staying home and working for Mother if you just simply could not face another day of school, homework, standing in line for lunch or math class with Mrs. Hanna. Some days it was better to go to school instead of mowing, chopping, digging and lifting, but the choice was yours. Mother would give you the option. The decision was up to you.

Life is a lot like deciding whether to go to school or work for Mother. Some days it pays to go to work, facing the most urgent and important tasks on your desk. Other days, you should forsake the regular work for a day of more creative endeavors. I don't mean take the day off and loaf, but there are days when you should be creative instead of focused on your "to do" list. The ability to choose what you work on is very important.

In his book, *How to Create a Mind: The Secret of Human Thought Revealed,* Ray Kurzweil talks about two modes of thinking. "One is *non-directed thinking,* in which thoughts trigger one another in a non-logical way. The second mode of thinking is *directed thinking,* which we use when we attempt to solve a problem or formulate an organized response."

I believe there are two types of work. *Non-directed work,* which is doing the routine, mundane thoughtless work that so many of

> *"Your purpose in life is to be creative."*
> Mary Monroe

us are caught up in every day. Then there is *directed work,* where we use every bit of our mental capacity to create something that no one has ever thought of before, like creating a new product or service.

Your purpose in life is to be creative. You are more valuable when you are creative. Employees who want to advance in their jobs need to focus on being more creative and advancement will take care of itself. Business owners who want to be more profitable need to focus on being more creative and the profits will come.

One of the greatest joys you can experience in life is when you are creative. To be creative is to be really alive. The purpose of human life is to create. Creativity is man's highest moral purpose.

When you align your purpose in life with your creative abilities, you will reach a state of harmony. That harmony comes from doing creative work. *The more you align your values, your actions, your purpose and your creative spirit, the more productive you become.* Energy flows to you and through you. Time seems to stand still. Hours can fly by without you even noticing (I have been writing for six hours!).

By living your own life to the fullest, you will be a shining example to others of what is possible. When others see you in your creative mode, they get to witness what life is supposed to be. Sharing your creative abilities with others is what celebrating life is all about. Sharing your creative abilities is how you teach others to celebrate their own life.

Don't resent others because they are more successful. Celebrate the people you find in your life and they will help you to discover the creative person within you. Rather than comparing yourself to others and resenting the creativity they have found, remain open and receptive to the creative genius within yourself. Allow that genius to be like the planting of a seed within you that, with nourishment, will grow into your own creative genius.

Riches flow to you when you are creative. Great riches flow to the most creative among us. Think of the greatest artists, musicians and writers. Creativity cannot be controlled by others. Creativity is a freedom that must be discovered within each of us; a freedom that has to be earned.

One of the days I chose to stay at home and work with Mother, we created a huge bed of flowers that was arranged into great sweeps of color. When we finished and stood back to examine our work, Mother said, "Life is like creating a beautiful flower bed. If you take the time to be creative in all that you do, it will show. Give your best every day and you will be a success. All work is creative work, whether it is planting pansies, refinishing a door, building a house or running a business. The highest moral purpose a person has in their life is to be creative."

Some days you have to go to school or work. Some days you should skip your normal routine and do the most creative work that you are capable of. When you find a way to do the work you love and get paid for it at the same time, you will have found your calling in life.

Today, if you don't want to go to school or to your job, take the day off and work with my Mother. I am sure she has a long list of things for you to do!

71

Stealing Dogwoods

"You have to be planted in the right spot to grow."
Mary Monroe

"Put all the shovels and rakes in the trunk of the car. Better get the ax, too. Make sure we have some burlap sacks and plastic to put the dogwoods on."

Mama never had a pickup truck so she moved bushes and trees in the trunk of her car. She needed a pickup truck today because we were going off the farm to dig up dogwood trees. Leaving the farm to work was always an adventure for a boy of eleven or twelve.

As the car swung onto Middle Road, I wondered where we were going. Mother drove to Rock Hill Road, off Old Dunn Road, about five miles from our house. She turned down a dirt road to the left, and after a few minutes slowed down and turned off that dirt road onto an old logging trail that was nothing more than two ruts with high grass in the middle. We made it about one hundred feet before the ruts ended and we had to stop in a small clearing of trees.

Then, out came the shovels and rakes, and we began to dig up little dogwood trees. It was amazing that Mother had found this place. Dogwood trees love living under the canopy of pine trees in North Carolina. Under the mature dogwood trees were lots of seedlings. These seedlings were about two feet tall and easy to dig. They came out of the ground with very little argument.

I thought it was amazing that in the fall of the year, Mother could tell the dogwoods from the other leafless trees in the woods, until I noticed brightly colored ribbons and pieces of yarn tied to the little trees. Mother had been here in the spring and marked the trees that she wanted. They would be transplanted to Mother's nursery, and then later distributed to her yard and the yards of others. As we dug, I realized that there was a lot of planning and effort put into keeping Mother's garden and yard beautiful.

After an hour of digging dogwoods and putting them in the trunk of the car, a truck rattled down the dirt road and slowed down as it passed us in the woods. Before the truck was out of sight it stopped suddenly, backed up rapidly to the logging trail and turned into the woods where we were.

Mother's face had an odd expression when she said, "Get the tools and put them in the trunk of the car. Close the trunk and get into the car and no matter what happens don't say a word!"

Well, it was rather scary to be spoken to in a voice that was not to be argued with, in a strange wood, with a truck approaching, and ordered to the car. As I put the shovels and rakes in the trunk of the car, the truck came to a stop beside me. I could see the man driving the truck, and he did not look happy. Something told me not to allow him to see how many dogwoods were in the car, so I closed the trunk quietly and got in the car on the passenger side. I did not dare look at him as he came past, but I could not help but hear the heated conversation that took place when he spoke to Mother. He was demanding to know what we were doing "on his property?" Mother was as polite as always, but I noticed she was a little vague with her answers.

The man was verbally attacking my Mother and I wanted to come to her rescue, but she had ordered me to the car and I did not know what to do. I was a small boy and he was a grown man, so I sat very still and listened. The argument lasted a few minutes and finally Mother was moving toward the car.

She got in, started the car and off we went toward home. There was silence as we went down Old Dunn Road and turned onto Dobbin Holmes Road. Finally, I could not stand the silence anymore and I had to ask, "Mama, what happened back there?"

"Well," she said slowly, "we just got caught stealing dogwoods!"

Oh my God, I was devastated. My mother was stealing dogwoods and leading me into a life of crime! I never thought of Mother as a thief and the concept did not sit very well with me. I always thought my parents were supposed to be law-abiding citizens. My mother could not be a thief, could she? After all, my parents were perfect weren't they? They were *my* parents!

She said, "Son, sometimes you have to break the rules if you want to change things for the better. I should have asked permission before we dug someone else's trees, but those dogwoods are being wasted down in the woods hidden like that. Those dogwoods were not in the right spot to grow. All we were doing was liberating them for other people to enjoy. It was really more like a rescue mission than stealing. If we left them in the woods, very few of them would have survived. Only a few of those seedlings would gain enough water, food and sunlight in that crowded wood to survive to maturity. We will take them back home and heal them behind the barn, and then transplant them into the perfect spot to grow. To grow, a bush or tree has to be planted in the right spot. Some bushes like shade while others like full sunshine. Some like sandy soil and some like rich black earth."

I pondered what Mother said as I transplanted those dogwoods behind the barn. People have to be planted in the right spot to grow, just like dogwood trees. Today, when I consult with businesses about how to improve productivity and get the most from the people they employ, my advice comes right from Mother, *"People have to be planted in the right spot to grow."*

> *"You have to be planted in the right spot to grow."*
> Mary Monroe

When you get the right people doing the right things in your business, your productivity will increase. You will have planted the right people in the right spots to grow. When you match the talent, creativity and love of someone to their work, everyone benefits.

The staff that I currently have working with me is an eclectic group of people who are as different from each other as they can possibly be, but together they form an amazingly talented group of creative people. One is obsessive compulsive and adheres to all the rules, so she takes fabulous care of our money. Another is so concerned with the happiness of everyone she meets that she has become the queen of customer service. Our technology genius is a wizard with computers, networks and hardware. Our graphics designer is lost in her computer most days, but when she designs something she can dazzle your eyes. Each of these people have been planted in the right spot so they can grow and be creative every day.

A lot of times, Mother had me plant a bush or tree in one spot, and then a year or two later she would say, "I don't think that bush likes it there. Let's move it." So I would dig it up and move it to a new home. Then a couple years later she'd say, "See. It's so much happier here. It had to be planted in the right spot to grow."

Life is all about finding the right spot for you to grow. Are you planted in the right spot? You may have to transplant yourself by moving your job, your home or your relationships to become successful. When you get yourself in the right spot, doing the right things, you will have planted the seeds of your own success. Like Mother said, *"You have to be planted in the right spot to grow."*

To change your life, you sometimes have to break the rules, but I really don't recommend you steal dogwoods. You might get caught!

Your "Is Done" Pile

"You have to know where you are,
to know where you are going."
Mary Monroe

It was a crystal clear, cool, fall day in North Carolina; one of those days you just had to get outside and play. Unfortunately for me, Mother had other ideas. That was the way it worked with Mother. Once she set her mind to something, it had to be done right then. There were fourteen bushes by the barn that needed to be moved, and today was moving day. I would be the muscle and Mother would be the brains. I would dig and Mother would make sure that each bush had the right amount of water, dirt and fertilizer to make it happy in its new home.

The bush moving process began with me digging fourteen holes in the ground. It was backbreaking, mindless work. There was nothing to think about but digging the holes wide and deep enough to satisfy Mother. She supervised the job and would tell me to make *this hole a little deeper* or *that one a little bigger*.

The really hard work began when I dug up the holly bushes to transplant. You start by digging a circle around the outside of the bush to make sure you don't cut any of its roots. Then you work the shovel under the bush very carefully to set it free. Finally, you can lift the bush from its hole after most of the dirt has been removed.

The holly bushes didn't like to be uprooted, so they put up a fight. Their leaves have thorns which scratched and pricked me everywhere. When I finally got the bush out of the ground there was a dirt and root ball on the bottom that weighed fifty pounds. I placed it in the wheelbarrow and pushed it to the new hole to replant.

Now, don't think that Mother was letting me do all the work. She was right there, digging and pulling on the bushes with me. Sometimes she would stop me so she could get down in the hole to make sure the bush was giving up its dirt, but not its roots. Then she would have me go back to digging. I got to do all the heavy work while she did all the thinking, which was fine with me. After what seemed like forever, she called for a water break, and while I rested and drank my water, Mother wandered around, looking at the holly bushes and the holes that were dug.

"What are you looking at?" I asked.

"I am looking at our 'Is Done Pile,'" she replied.

"Our what pile?"

"Our 'Is Done Pile.' When you work, you must always stop and look at what you have accomplished. *You have to know where you are, to know where you are going.* You can see how far you have come and what you have left to do. You can estimate the time it will take to finish based on what you have already completed. Stopping to look at your 'Is Done Pile' allows you to evaluate the partially completed work and see if you are going in the right direction. You can detect problems and correct them before it is too late. But most importantly, you get to enjoy the accomplishment of the work you have done so far. Your 'Is Done Pile' is the way you get the most out of any project. Now get back to digging!"

Over the years, I have thought about what Mother said many times, and I realized that in life and business you need to stop from time to time and look at your "Is Done Pile." You can see how far you have come and what you have left to do. You can estimate the time it will take to finish based on what you have already completed. Stopping to look at your "Is Done Pile" allows you to evaluate the partially completed work and see if you are going in the right direction. You can detect problems and correct them before it is too late. But most important, you get to enjoy the accomplishment of the work you have done so far. All in all, stopping to look at your "Is Done Pile" is a great way to get the most out of life.

> *"You have to know where you are, to know where you are going."*
> Mary Monroe

The process of reviewing your "Is Done Pile" is the key to life and business planning. Most people don't have a plan to guide their life or business. They figure that all they have to do is work hard every day and somehow they will succeed. To be successful you must focus on the important activities that will move you toward your goals. Take time every day to consider your goals and to determine the most important things you must focus on to accomplish them. *You have to know where you are, to know where you are going.*

You should set yearly and monthly goals to put your feet on the right path. You should plan each week to make sure you are accomplishing the things that will lead you to your goals. You should prioritize each day to make sure you are focused on the most important tasks. Let the unimportant things remain undone; they are unimportant.

After learning about my "Is Done Pile," I began to evaluate things differently. In school, all I had to do was stop and look at the homework I had already accomplished and I would know what was possible. Today in my business, when projects seem too big, I simply stop and look at my 'Is Done Pile.' I take time to review my progress on a regular basis to evaluate where I am, where I am going, and if the path I am on will get me where I want to go.

This lesson helped me finish this book. Many times during the writing of this book, I have become discourages and felt like it would never be completed. Then I would look at the piles of pages that were complete and it made me realize that I was making progress toward my goal. As you read this completed book, you are holding my "Is Done Pile."

Mother always said, *"You have to know where you are, to know where you are going."*

When Mother and I finished moving all the bushes, we stood back and admired our work. It had been a difficult day, but when we saw what we had accomplished, we realized that the job had been worth our efforts.

Take time to enjoy the "Is Done Pile" of your life, and then Mother would tell you to, "Get back to digging!"

Raining Rabbits

"Success does not create happiness;
happiness creates success."
The Happiness Advantage by Shawn Achor

It was the middle of the summer and a thunderstorm had blown up, dumping buckets of rain on an otherwise great day. The electricity was knocked out by the storm and there was nothing to do, nobody to play with, and I was bored. I would never say I was bored out loud because if I told Mother, she would find work for me.

I sat in the big red chair in the living room, staring out the window. The weather was clearing, but not fast enough for me. The rain was still coming down lightly and there were rolls of thunder rumbling around. The setting sun was peeking out from under the edge of the storm, casting a wonderful glow on our back yard.

Suddenly, I noticed a huge, brown, cotton-tailed rabbit sitting perfectly still in the back yard, close to the house. I watched him in fascination because rabbits very rarely came out in the daytime. The rabbit knew that during the storm the kids were in the house and our dog Barky would be napping in his corner of the carport.

That rabbit sat perfectly still for a few minutes, and then without warning he exploded from his spot and sprinted across the yard. I have never seen a rabbit move faster in a straight line than that rabbit did that day. As suddenly as he had started, the rabbit stopped running, lay over on his side and slid about twenty feet in the soft, wet grass. At the end of his slide, he righted himself like a baseball player sliding into second base and sat perfectly still, panting for breath. In a few moments he took off running again across the yard, built up speed and slid to a stop. The big fat rabbit did his run and slide routine again and again. He was playing in the wet grass of the back yard! You could almost see him smiling.

"Success does not create happiness; happines creates success."
The Happiness Advantage
by Shawn Achor

I never thought of wild animals playing, but over the years, I have witnessed it many times. Hawks turning lazy circles in the sky becomes a game when they pitch and scream at each other. Horses nip and chase in the pasture, kittens will wait to attack each other from behind a corner. Dogs will chase and wrestle each other to the ground. I have watched two grey foxes playing with a tennis ball by pouncing on it, grabbing it in their mouth, shaking their head and letting it fly, only to chase it down and pounce on it again.

Play is whatever absorbs us fully, creates purpose and order, and involves us in a meaningful interaction. Children will create elaborate imaginary games, and play in their fantasy world for hours where a stick becomes a sword and a cardboard box becomes a house. Play is fun, and scientists tell us that play is how we learn.

Shawn Achor has studied happiness for years and has written a book called *The Happiness Advantage: Linking Positive Brains to Performance.* His book demonstrates the wisdom of playing and having fun. He says, "Happiness is not on the other side of success. Success does not create happiness, happiness creates success."

According to Achor, happy people absorb information quicker and are 31% more productive than unhappy people. Happy people turn on all the learning centers in their brain. Achor's research shows happiness does not occur when we reach our goals. Most of us set goals and think that we will be happy when we achieve them. Once we have achieved the goal we set, we set a new goal and strive to achieve happiness once again.

Achor believes that you can train your brain to be happy, and he has measured the results of a simple daily routine that will improve your happiness and your productivity. He says you should do the following things each day for a month to see a difference in your life.

1. Every day identify three things you are grateful for.
2. Daily write about a positive experience in your journal.
3. Exercise every day to teach your brain that behavior matters.
4. Daily practice meditation or prayer that focuses on quieting the mind, which helps you accomplish more and be more positive.
5. Daily create random acts of kindness by sending one positive email, a hand written note to someone you know or buy a stranger's lunch anonymously.

Mother would add fun to the things she taught us so we did not notice we were learning. She served milk to her grandchildren from a small pitcher that looked like a cow. She would serve her famous blackberry jelly in tiny jars to her grandchildren. She would greet you at the door when you came home from school with a "sweet potato ice cream cone," which was simply a small sweet potato with the skin torn off and butter melting on the top that looked like an ice cream cone. She was teaching us to eat good food instead of junk food.

As a speaker, I have learned that if I can keep the audience laughing, they will learn ten times faster. Humor causes endorphins to be pumped into your brain, which heightens awareness and speeds up learning.

Practice Shawn Achor's five steps for the next thirty days and see if you are happier. Remember that, *success does not create happiness; happiness creates success.* Be happy and success will flow to you.

Cleaning the Gutters

*"Everything you do in life prepares
you to do something else."*

Mother always chose Thanksgiving Day for me to clean out
the gutters on our house. I never understood why she chose that
day until years later, when my sisters told me that Mother was
simply trying to keep me out of the kitchen so she could cook
Thanksgiving dinner in peace.

We had a huge water oak tree in the back yard that was hundreds of years old, and in the fall of the year, the leaves fell like
rain. Those oak leaves were small enough to fill up the gutters,
and they had to be removed so the winter rains could run into the
drainpipe. Cleaning the gutters was too big of a job for a twelve
year old boy, but Mother said I had to do it, so I did. Besides, anytime you can climb up on the roof of the house, it is an exciting
day.

First I had to assemble my tools. The ladder, gloves to protect
my hands, a rake for the leaves on the roof, a broom to sweep the
roof, a hose to wash out the gutters, and a sandwich in case I got
hungry. There is something magical about sitting on the roof of
your house and eating a sandwich.

The initial climb to the roof was always scary. The most dangerous point comes when you leave the ladder to obtain a foot-
hold on the roof. Once you are on the roof, everything calms
down. The roof of our one-story house was not very steep or that

far from the ground, so moving around was fairly simple. Standing on the roof of our house was like standing on the top of the world. Everything looked so different from up there. It felt like I could see forever! The horses in the pasture looked smaller, and I could see my cousins playing in their yard across the road. Life was great. I was on top of the world. I was doing a job that was too big for me.

Then, I had to listen to the pre-job briefing from Mother about not falling off the roof and breaking my neck. Mother had never been on the roof of our house, but none of that stopped her from standing in the yard and lobbing advice up to me once I was on the roof. "Don't move too fast, you might slip. Don't get too close to the edge. Always hang on with one hand and work with the other one. Don't go over the crest of the house without letting me know."

> *"Everything you do in life prepares you to do something else."*

It amazed me how I was supposed to follow Mother's instructions and still clean out the gutters. I had to move about the roof, so I could not sit still. I had to get to the edge of the roof, because that is where the gutters were. I had to use both hands to dig the compacted leaves out of the gutters. After she left the yard and was not watching any more, I decided that some of her advice was simply not feasible. I decided that only after she was back in the house and could not see me.

At twelve years old, I should not have been allowed to climb up on the roof to clean out the gutters. It was too big of a job for a young man, but doing a job that was entirely too big for me was the point! Taking your life in your own hands and moving around on the roof without your mother being able to stop you was fabulous. It taught me that you can accomplish anything you set your mind to. It taught me that *everything you do in life prepares you to do something else.*

Later in life, when I was asked to do things that I knew were too big for me, I would think about cleaning out the gutters and knew I could do it. I knew that I could accomplish tasks that were beyond my capabilities because I already had. Difficult tasks became simple when you compare them to cleaning out the gutters. Today, I am always doing things I don't know how to do. That is how I get to do them.

In our protective society today, young people are not asked to go beyond their capabilities enough. We protect them, keep them from harm, and keep them well within their limits. If a child grows up and does not exceed their limits from time to time, they never know what they are capable of.

Running the farm, raising four children without a husband, starting businesses, getting involved in politics, and most everything else Mother did, was a job that was too big for her, but she did it anyway. She knew that she had to become more than she was if she was going to be successful.

I had to be careful on the edge of the roof when I was cleaning the gutters so I would not fall. Mother had to be careful with the edges of her life (with money and business), because one mistake might cause her to fail. We both had to learn to do a job that was too big for us.

When was the last time you took on a task that was too big for you? When was the last time you took a risk? Without risk, there is no reward. Without risk, you will never be able to stand on the roof of your house and see the world differently.

Weeks after I finished cleaning the gutters, I would look up at the roof and remember what it felt like to stand up there and accomplish a task that grown men are supposed to tackle. I remember Mother saying, *"Everything you do in life prepares you to do something else."*

It was a good feeling to know that I had accomplished a task bigger than I was. It was like standing on the top of the world.

LESSON 4
How Money Works

Mary Monroe and her granddaughter, Kristin Hill
1980's

Money is...

"Money is frozen productive work."
Mary Monroe

When Mother wanted something done on the farm, sometimes she would pay me a fixed price for the job instead of paying me by the hour. One day she asked what I would charge to cut down a tree. I surveyed the job and determined that I could cut it down, limb it up and haul it off in two hours. Hourly wages at the time were $3.60 per hour so I offered to do the job for twenty dollars and she accepted.

It took one hour of work to cut the tree down and cut all the limbs off. I was feeling pretty good about the deal I had struck, when Mother came by and asked, "What are you going to do with all the money you are earning?"

My mind began to whirl with all the possibilities of spending the money, and then she asked, "Do you know what that money really is?

"Money is frozen productive work. The twenty dollars you are earning is your own hard work frozen into a piece of paper. Money is a tool, just like the ax you used to cut down this tree. When you work and earn money, you are turning that work into a piece of paper. *The money in your wallet is your frozen productive work.* You can take that paper to the grocery store and trade it for a loaf of bread. The money you pay for bread represents the frozen productive work of the baker who produced it.

"Money is a tool of exchange. The purpose of a tool is to do productive work. The purpose of money is to freeze your hard work so you can trade it for the hard work of others. Money enables you to trade your best efforts for the best efforts of others so that each of you can do the type of work you love. Money demands that you trade the absolute best that is within you for the best someone else has to offer."

And with the statement of *"money is frozen productive work"* ringing in my ears, Mother wandered off and allowed me to think. I was earning money cutting down the tree, but was I really going to blow my hard work for a hamburger on Friday night?

When I speak to audiences about creating wealth, I ask the attendees to finish this sentence, "Money is ...?"

I get lots of responses: Money is Freedom, Needed, Power, Status, Importance, Reward, Distraction, Necessary, A key source of support, Lifestyle. Before the exercise is over someone from the audience will always say, "Money is the root of all evil." We are all familiar with that statement which came from thousands of years ago when slave labor was used to produce wealth. I wonder if you ever asked yourself, "What is the root of money?"

One of Mother's favorite books was *Atlas Shrugged,* by Ayn Rand. It holds one of the best explanations of what money is that I have ever read. Here is what Ayn Rand has to say about money:

"Money is a tool of exchange, which can't exist unless there are goods produced and men able to produce them. Money is the

material shape of the principle that men who wish to deal with one another must deal by trade and give value for value."

The American free enterprise system allows men and women to produce valuable products they can trade for the valuable products of others. Do you consider that system of free trade evil?

"Money is made possible only by the men who produce. When you accept money in payment for your effort, you do so only on the conviction that you will exchange it for the product of the effort of others."

Do you consider your efforts evil? Do you think that trading your best effort for the best effort of others is evil?

"Money is frozen productive work."
Mary Monroe

"Not an ocean of tears nor all the guns in the world can transform those pieces of paper in your wallet into the bread you will need to survive tomorrow. Those pieces of paper, which should have been gold, are a token of honor - your claim upon the energy of the men who produce."

Will you exchange your efforts (your money), for an inferior product? Not if you have choices. The only economic system on earth that gives you those choices is the free enterprise system or Capitalism.

"..Man's mind is the root of all the goods produced and of all the wealth that has ever existed on earth.

"Wealth is the product of man's capacity to think. Then is money made by the man who invents a motor at the expense of those who did not invent it? Is money made by the intelligent at the expense of the fools? By the able at the expense of the incompetent? By the ambitious at the expense of the lazy? Money is made; made by the effort of every honest man, each to the extent of his ability."

Money is created by your capacity to think, to learn new skills, and to take action. Money must be made before it can be spent. Economic systems since the beginning of time have prevented people from creating wealth. Money was given to you by the king, or your title, or you were born into money or poverty with no ability to change your station in life. The United States is the first country that is based on an economic system where wealth can be created. In the American free enterprise system you can start out a pauper and become the richest man or woman in the county, just ask Oprah or Bill Gates.

"If you ask me to name the proudest distinction of Americans, I would choose - because it contains all the others - the fact that they were the people who created the phrase 'to make money' ...Americans were the first to understand that wealth has to be created. The words 'to make money' hold the essence of human morality."

Money is your claim upon the productive energy of others. As long as you are *free to trade* your productive energy, those pieces of paper we call money will transform themselves into the bread that you need to eat. But only when you are free to trade will money work. Money is based on a society of free people who trade based on private property rights.

"But money is only a tool. It will take you wherever you wish, but it will not replace you as the driver. It will give you the means for the satisfaction of your desires, but it will not provide you with desires."

"Money will not purchase happiness for the man who has no concept of what he wants: money will not give him a code of values, if he's evaded the knowledge of what to value, and it will not provide him with a purpose, if he's evaded the choice of what to seek. Money will not buy intelligence for the fool, or admiration for the coward, or respect for the incompetent."

Money, and the free trade it represents, is the root of all the good in the world. When men and women are free to trade their best efforts for the best efforts of others, society prospers.

"Money demands that you sell, not your weakness to men's stupidity, but your talent to their reason; it demands that you buy, not the shoddiest they offer, but the best that your money can find. And when men live by (free) trade - with reason, not force, as their final arbiter - it is the best product that wins, the best performance, the man of the best judgment and highest ability - and the degree of a man's productiveness is the degree of his reward."

After Mother explained how money worked, I became conscious of how hard I had to work to make money and the value it represented in my life. After that tree was completely cut down, limbed up, and hauled to the burning pile, I had a great sense of accomplishment and twenty dollars that represented my hard work, too!

Now I understand what Mother meant when she said, *"Money is frozen productive work."*

Poor, Rich and Wealthy People

"It is your choices that define you, not your abilities."
Mary Monroe

When I was building Cloverfield Tennis and Swim Club, I hired a worker named Joe to help me. Every Friday afternoon when paycheck time came he would say, "Will you take me to the bank so I can get it cashed? Then will you take me downtown to the pool hall?"

I would say, "Joe, please don't spend all of your money this weekend."

Every weekend he spent all his money on "wine, women and song," as the saying goes. This man's behavior was so odd to me that I asked Mother if it was typical of most people. Mother said, "There are three types of people; poor people, rich people and wealthy people. Each one is determined by the choices they make."

She said, "Poor people believe that money is earned to be spent. They are poor because they choose to spend their money as soon as they get it. Rich people earn more money than poor people, but they believe that money is earned to be spent and choose to spend their money as soon as they get it. Rich people have a big house, expensive car, fancy country club and all the things that they think rich people are supposed to have. Rich people have huge expenses and huge debt. If they lose their job or source of income, they will be poor very soon. There is no real philosophical difference between rich people and poor people. Rich people just spend money at a higher volume than poor people, but they think in the same way. Both believe that money is earned to be spent.

"Wealthy people have a completely different belief about money. They understand that money is frozen productive work. They understand that money is a tool of trade. Wealthy people know that the purpose of money, like any tool, is to produce. It doesn't matter how much money wealthy people earn, they simply spend less than they take in and invest the difference into income producing assets that create more money."

Mother said, "You must choose which type of person you want to be. *It is your choices that define you, not your abilities.* The choices you make determine whether you are poor, rich or wealthy. Our self-discipline determines the outcome of our economic status. I certainly hope you make the right choices."

> *"It is your choices that define you, not your abilities."*
> Mary Monroe

I spent years thinking about what mother said, and seeking wealthy people who could be role models for me. Albert McCauley, who grew up down Middle Road from our house, became one of those role models. He barely graduated high school and somehow made it into the University of North Carolina at Chapel Hill. In his first semester a professor told him to go home because he "was not college material," and at the end of his first semester, he left school.

Albert went to work for his father's moving and storage company while he and a good friend, Kenny McDonald, tried to figure out how to make extra money. They opened a small convenience store on Person Street between the coin operated laundry and the liquor store. It was a rough part of town.

That store made money so they opened another one and it made money, too. Over the years, they opened lots of convenience stores. A few years ago they sold all of their convenience stores for millions of dollars. Albert is now one of the wealthiest men I know. Albert is also on the Board of Directors for Methodist University Business School. I guess he is "college material" after all.

The size of your paycheck doesn't matter; it matters what you do with it. What part of your earnings you are going to invest in your financial future? Do you want to be poor, rich or wealthy?

Remember what Mother said, *"It is your choices that define you, not your abilities."*

Haircuts on the Porch

"Wealthy people and poor people get their
haircuts at home, but for different reasons."
Mary Monroe

Mother worked as a hairdresser early in her life, and she cut my hair on the front porch of our house until I was forty years old. She would put an old shower curtain around my shoulders and hold it in place with two clothespins. Then she would cut my hair and discuss business or politics while she had a captive audience.

She would say, "Son, if you get your haircut at a barber shop or beauty salon it will cost twenty dollars. That is forty dollars a month, four hundred eighty a year and four thousand eight hundred in ten years."

I had forty years of haircuts on the front porch saving me over nineteen thousand dollars.

Wealthy people and poor people both get their haircuts at home, but for different reasons. Poor people squander their money on unimportant things and so they don't have enough money left for a haircut. They *have* to get their hair cut at home. Wealthy people spend a lifetime choosing to use their money to create wealth and they have enough money to *afford the luxury* of having their hair cut at home.

Mother did not spend money on unimportant things. We drank water from Welch's Fred Flintstone Jelly jars, our birthday cards were recycled from the last year and when we went shopping, Mother made us drink from a water fountain instead of purchasing bottled water or a Coke. We did not eat dinner out when Mother could cook.

But Mother never skimped when it came to purchasing the important things. She bought the best quality products and services that she could afford. We were sent to private schools to get the best education possible. We all had cars and houses. Mother started several of us in business, but I still got my haircuts on the front porch. By controlling her spending on little things, Mother was able to have money for the important things.

Mother's ways to reduce spending and create wealth are simple and require only one thing: self-discipline.

1. **Calculate your monthly expenses.** Take the time to calculate the monthly cost for operating your household. The self-discipline required to set a budget and follow it is a sure path to wealth. Sit down with your family and explain your income and expenses. Once your financial situation is understood by your entire family, everyone will spend less money. You must teach your children about money; they will not learn it anywhere else.

2. **Create a weekly spending log** by writing down every penny you spend and what you spent it on. You will be amazed where your money is going.

3. **Stop paying for things that are almost free** like water, coffee, tea and snacks. Bring them with you from home.

4. Use cash not debit cards. When you use cash for purchases you will be aware of what you are spending. If you don't have the cash to make the purchase, DON'T BUY IT! It builds self-discipline to spend only the money that you have.

5. Eliminate *all* your credit card debt, NOW!! Credit cards are the most popular way to "have your money and spend it too!" A credit card is not money; it is a promise that you will pay money later, with interest.

6. Purchase used cars. The typical new car loses fifteen to twenty percent of its value from the time you buy it until you drive off the auto dealer's lot. Purchase cars that are one or two years old with very low mileage. You get a car that is "new" to you and save the depreciation.

7. Eliminate debts. Car sickness is the feeling you get when the car payment is due! Simply eliminating debt, like a car payment, will improve your financial position. Work to eliminate one debt at a time until you are free and clear of all debt. Once that car is paid off, do not run out and purchase another one!

8. Cook more - eat out less. Eating out is a treat that we all enjoy, but for the cost of a meal eaten in a restaurant you can feed your family for several days. Pack your leftovers for lunch the next day. Take the time to plan meals for your family, and then treat yourself to an occasional dinner out.

9. Spend money on important things. Food, shelter and clothing are the necessities of life. Stopping by the coffee shop for a four dollar cup of coffee you could have made at home for four cents is not. Ask yourself before you spend money, "Is this a necessary and important purchase?" If it is not, you can do without it!

10. **Reduce your tax bill** by consulting a tax advisor or CPA.

11. **Pay your own bills with checks.** Writing checks will make you aware of your actual expenses. Balance your checkbook every month so you know where your money is going.

12. **Spend less than you earn** so you will have money left over for saving and investing in your future financial independence.

My niece, Kristin, majored in economics at Wake Forest University. When she turned twenty-one years old, she received a Happy Birthday card from Mother with twenty-one dollars in it, which was Mother's typical birthday gift. The card was an old Happy Anniversary card that Mother had scratched out the "Anniversary" and written "Birthday" instead. Kristin's roommate thought the card was horrible. "Couldn't your grandmother afford a real card?" she groaned.

"You don't understand my grandmother, Honey." Kristin replied. "She would never spend money on unimportant things like a card. She would rather spend money on an economics degree from Wake Forest!"

Today, Kristin and her husband have three young children, and they spend money on important things. Oh, their kids don't want for a single thing, but Kristin doesn't spend money on frivolous things. I bet she even cuts her boys' hair herself, on the front porch with a shower curtain wrapped around them, held together with a clothespin.

Mother's Coconut Cake

"You can't have your cake and eat it too."
Mary Monroe

Mother made the most amazing coconut cake. She would buy a fresh coconut, crack it open and drain the juice before removing the meat and grating it by hand. She used the fresh coconut juice to pour over the cake so it would penetrate the cake layers and the entire thing would become a gastronomic delight. For my birthday, I always requested a coconut cake. When I would get down to one last piece, I would say, "I wish I had more cake."

Mother would say, "You can't have your cake and eat it too."

Mother taught us that there is no mystical, magical way to *have your cake and eat it too.* She taught that you cannot fake reality if you are going to live on this planet. Sooner or later you have to face the reality you live in. Mother lived by what Aristotle believed, "A is A." A thing is itself. A stone cannot be a stone and a tree at the same time. Money works the same way as Mama's coconut cake. You cannot have your money and spend it too. You can only eat your cake once. *You can only spend your money once.*

At some point, most people attempt to spend money that they don't have by borrowing money or using credit cards to purchase what they have not earned. You cannot consume more than you earn. Nobody can spend money and keep it, too. No matter how much you want it, you cannot have your cake and eat it, too.

Here are Mother's Rules for Creating Wealth:

1. Make choices daily about spending money. When you want to purchase something, ask yourself if you should spend your money this way.

2. Rich people don't work for their money; their money works for them.

3. Choose your friends carefully; you will learn from them. Successful friends talk about successful activities. Listen and learn.

4. Invest in yourself first, and then pay your monthly bills. Save ten percent of your income to build your financial independence. This will create the self-discipline necessary to become wealthy.

5. Hire your brains by trusting the advice of your CPA, attorney, or REALTOR®.

6. When investing ask, "How long before I get my money back?"

7. Work to *learn,* not just to *earn.* If you want to achieve some thing in your life, start working in that field to learn how the masters do it. Your life will improve when you know a little about a lot of things.

8. Your most powerful asset is your mind. Use it constantly!

9. Your house is your largest investment. Work hard to get it paid for. One third of the houses in America are paid for free and clear.

10. Wealthy people purchase income-producing assets, not things. Assets put money in your pocket. Liability takes money out of your pocket.

I was asked to examine the business of a very successful businesswoman and advise her on building wealth. She had thirteen employees, her own TV show, magazine and limousine. She owned her own home but it was mortgaged to the hilt. She owned a beach house but the mainte-

> *"You can't have your cake and eat it too."*
> Mary Monroe

nance and homeowner's dues cost her so much that she could have rented the penthouse in the nicest hotel anytime and spent less money. She drove a huge Mercedes, but the payment on the car was over one thousand dollars per month.

Her business was grossing about two million dollars per year. She had no investments, and her fixed business expenses were sixty seven thousand dollars per month. She only took home about one hundred thousand dollars a year after all expenses. When I analyzed her business, I discovered that she was spending all the money she took in just to run her business!

I advised her how to reduce her expenses, spend less than she earned and become wealthy by purchasing income-producing real estate. She listened politely, but would not make any changes.

To her, being a rock star in her industry was more exciting than creating wealth. It has been ten years since I worked with this lady and I checked on her recently. She is still known as a celebrity in her industry, but is no closer to being wealthy than she was ten years ago. She will not become wealthy unless she changes her beliefs about money. She is still eating her cake and trying to have it, too.

Wealth is based on a simple philosophical principle that you cannot consume more than you produce, or as Mother would say, *"You cannot have your cake and eat it, too."*

Just make my cake, coconut.

Here is Mother's recipe for coconut cake, in case you would like to try it.

COCONUT CAKE
1 package (12 oz.) fresh coconut (or grate your own fresh)
1 cup sugar
1/2 cup milk
3 butter cake layers
Comfort icing (boiled icing or 7-minute frosting)
2 egg whites
3/4 cup granulated sugar
2/3 cup white Karo syrup
1 tsp. cream of tarter
1 tsp. vanilla
2 tbsp. water
Dash of salt

Bake three cake layers using the 1-2-3-4 Butter Cake recipe.

FILLING: Combine sugar, milk, and ¾ coconut in a medium saucepan. Heat just to a boil and immediately remove. Pour a little of this filling on the top of the middle and bottom layers.

FROSTING: In a double boiler, combine egg whites, granulated sugar, white Karo syrup, vanilla, cream of tartar, water, and salt. Constantly beat ingredients at high speed with a handheld mixer for about seven minutes, or until stiff peaks begin to form. Before icing becomes too stiff, spread on top and all around the sides of prepared cake. Cover icing with fresh coconut. On a rainy day, do not add as much coconut and icing around sides of cake or it will slide.

Notes written by Mother: The seven minute icing used for this cake was named "Temper Icing" by my children. They gave it this name because the seven minutes of mixing over a hot stove always seemed to get right on my last nerve!

Debt Is Constant. Income Is Variable.

"Are you robbing Peter to pay Paul?"
Mary Monroe

In the 1960's, my father loaned ten thousand dollars to a man to start a hardware store, which was a huge sum of money at that time. After father died, Mother discovered the loan and contacted the man to ask when she could expect payment. His reply was, "I owed that money to L.A. Monroe, not you. I have no intention of ever repaying that loan." Mother was devastated to learn the man had so little integrity that he would refuse to repay a loan to a widowed woman raising four children.

Mother recommended that her children never borrow money. She would say that "debt is constant and income is variable." Mother was a good teacher, but I did not listen closely enough.

I started Cloverfield Tennis and Swim Club, Inc., my first corporation, when I was 21 years old. My brother-in-law and I bought the land, built a clubhouse, tennis courts and a fabulous swimming pool on 13 acres of land. We invested what money we had saved and borrowed the rest to start the business. That debt was huge, and the principal and interest payment was three thousand three hundred dollars every single month!

I ran that business for ten years and every penny of the profit I made went to the bank to make the mortgage payment. Those ten years of struggling to pay the bank every month taught Mother's valuable lesson. *Debt is constant. Income is variable.* Income fluctuates over time as jobs come and go, or business profits fluctuate with consumer demand. Over time, income changes but debt is always there.

Mother taught us that all kinds of debt are bad, but the worst kind of debt is credit card debt. Credit card interest rates can be as high as 29%, and the credit card company can change your interest rate at any time without notice. Credit cards allow banks to collect large amounts of interest on small amounts of debt. You will never pay off a credit card debt if you just pay the minimum payment.

If you have five housand dollars in credit card debt with twelve percent annual interest rate, you will pay six hundred dollars in interest in a year. All debts are paid in after-tax dollars. You must earn eight thousand dollars to pay off that five thousand six hundred dollars credit card bill after federal and state income taxes and Social Security.

Another bad type of debt is the second mortgage or home equity line of credit. A second mortgage extracts the equity you have built up in your house to spend on other purchases. My neighbor borrowed fifty thousand on a second mortgage on his house to purchase a new truck. He took out a thirty year loan against his home to purchase a vehicle that will be almost worthless in five years. You should never pay interest on a depreciating liability like a vehicle.

As an active real estate agent during the real estate boom of the early 2000's, I saw firsthand the financial insanity that was created by Fannie Mae and Freddie Mac's lowering of the restrictions to borrowing money on home mortgages. Fannie Mae and Freddie Mac allowed No Document loans, which required no verification of job, salary or debts. We saw interest-only loans where the borrower repaid only interest, and not any principal on the loan.

Mother was right when she taught us that income is variable and debt is constant. Here are Mother's rules for managing debt:

- All your debt payments should not exceed 35% of your monthly income.

- Your home mortgage payment of Principal + Interest + Taxes + Insurance (PITI) should not exceed more than 25% of your total monthly income.

- You should have enough cash in savings to pay all your household bills for the next six months.

- You should never borrow against your home to buy cars or any other depreciating liability.

"Are you robbing Peter to pay Paul?"
Mary Monroe

My mother would tell you that if you cannot pay for it, don't buy it! The way to wealth is not borrow now and repay later. You cannot spend your way out of debt. The peaceful feeling of having your financial house in order is worth its weight in gold.

I got into financial trouble at one point in my life by not following Mother's advice. I had to borrow money from a family member to cover my debts. Before Mother died, she made me promise to repay that loan, no matter what it took. Repaying that loan took several years and was one of the most difficult things I have ever done in my life. I made a promise to Mother that I would repay it, and I did.

I learned firsthand that Mother was right when she said, *"Debt is constant. Income is variable."*

The Tax Man Cometh

"The taxpayer: That's someone who works for
the federal government, but doesn't have to take
the civil service examination."
President Ronald Reagan

It was one of those crystal clear October days that make you glad you live in North Carolina. Mother was holding court on her front porch with all her children in attendance, when a white car came rolling slowly down the long gravel driveway. We could tell that the car did not belong in our little community, and when it got close enough to read the official seal on the passenger door, we realized it was from the Cumberland County Tax Collectors Office.

An official looking county employee got out of the car and greeted us all warmly as he approached the porch. He asked if this was the residence of someone that none of us knew. After thanking us, he got back in his car and left. As soon as he was out of sight Mother said, "Whew! I thought he was here looking for me because I have not paid my property taxes for this year. Those taxes became due in September but are not past due until January first, so I never pay them until January. They don't give you a bonus for paying your taxes early."

Suddenly we were all confessing that no one had paid their property taxes and each one of us thought the tax man had come for us. Mother taught us to never pay taxes before they are due. She also taught us that taxes are the largest expense you have every year.

Most people don't think of taxes as an expense. Taxes are taken out of your paycheck before you receive it and you do not miss what you never had. If you were paid your entire salary and had to write a check back to the Internal Revenue Service every week, you would be much more aware of the taxes you pay.

The payment of taxes is a huge burden on Americans. Approximately one-third of our income goes to pay state, federal, and social security taxes. If you may make fifty thousand dollars a year you will pay about fifteen thousand dollars in taxes and only take home about thirty five thousand dollars. If you want to buy an item that costs seventy dollars, you have to earn one hundred dollars, and pay thirty dollars in taxes to have seventy dollars left over to purchase your item. You pay taxes on the money you earn before you get to spend it.

Every time private individuals trade, the government takes a piece. Uncle Adrian said that if four people stood in a circle and passed a ten dollar bill around, and the government took 30 percent in taxes from everyone as it changed hands, there would be nothing left when it came to the fourth person. Taxes would have taken it all!

In addition to income taxes, there are sales taxes, gasoline taxes, property taxes, dog taxes, fishing taxes, food taxes, hotel taxes, school taxes, and a host of other taxes hidden in everything you purchase. According to a study done at University of California, Berkeley, thirty-five percent of the cost of a house comes in the form of tax.

Here are some tax reduction strategies from my accountant, Brent Sumner, CPA. Before you take any steps to reduce your taxes, you should consult with your financial advisor or CPA. A great way to reduce taxes is to own a small business and some of these will apply only to small business owners. These tax reduction strategies apply in 2016 for the United States. I hope they are still around when you are reading this book.

1. **Home Sale Deduction:** You can sell your principal residence and pay no tax on the profit you make up to two hundred fifty thousand dollars for a single person and five hundred thousand dollars for a married couple. You must have lived in the house as your principal residence for two of the last five years. Prop erty taxes are also deductible on your principal residence.

2. **Individual Retirement Plans:** Retirement plans allow you to shelter income from taxes while you invest for your retirement. It is a great way to pay less tax and build financial independence in pretax dollars.

3. **Car Expenses:** If you use your automobile for business or charity, you can deduct the cost of operating your vehicle from your taxes, based on the amount your vehicle was used for the business or charity. You can use the actual expenses, including depreciation, or deduct the IRS allowance on a per mile basis. Whatever method you use must remain in effect throughout your ownership of the automobile.

4. **1031 Like Kind Exchange:** If you own property which is held for *investment purposes,* you can sell it and buy another

piece of "like kind property" without paying capital gains tax. This applies to equipment and real estate. To handle the transaction, you should use a professional 1031 Like-Kind Exchange Company instead of your personal CPA or tax attorney. See your CPA or tax attorney before beginning a like-kind exchange to see if it is the right move for you.

5. **Tuition Credits:** The IRS allows you a tuition credit paid for education. It is better to deduct the cost of a business education course as a normal business expense rather than take it as a tuition credit.

6. **Depreciation:** Your small business can depreciate business assets that you purchased to use in your business, like computers, cameras, copiers, etc. The most popular asset may be a truck or Sport Utility Vehicle that weighs in excess of six thousand pounds that you bought to use in your business.

7. **Hire Family Members:** Your children can work for your business and be paid a limited amount of wages without incurring any income or social security tax. (Approximately four thousand dollars - five thousand dollars per year.) Your children must actually work in your business, and you must be able to verify their hours and tasks. You can hire your child to do anything that helps your business, like wash your company car, address envelopes and manage your social media.

8. **Health Insurance:** One hundred precent of the cost of health insurance is deductible for small business owners.

9. **Business Meals, Entertainment and Travel:** Meals, entertainment and travel are deductible from your taxes as long as they are combined with a legitimate business meeting or trip. The percentage of the trip that is business is deductible from the total cost of the trip. Keep your receipts and document your business expenses.

10. **Use LLC's To Own Rental Properties:** An LLC is a great way to own rental properties.

11. **Unlimited Rental Losses for Real Estate Professionals:** Real estate professionals can deduct unlimited passive losses on investment real estate. You don't have to be a licensed REALTOR® to qualify. The standard IRS limit of twenty five thousand dollars does not apply to real estate professionals. See your CPA or tax attorney to see if you qualify.

My wife says that tax saving strategies are similar to a department store coupon. If your favorite store sent you a coupon to save fifty dollars, you must obey the rules stated on the coupon. Is there an expiration date, details of what merchandise is included, or a minimum purchase amount? The IRS sets the same type of exclusions, monetary limits, and date requirements to the tax saving "coupons" available to you and your business. Your accountant will clip all the coupons applicable to you, but you must

> *"The taxpayer:*
> *That's someone who works*
> *for the federal government*
> *but doesn't have to take*
> *the civil service examination."*
> *President Ronald Reagan*

follow the rules to save on taxes.

Sit down with your accountant to discuss tax saving strategies. Accounting is their passion and they know all the ways to save you money on taxes.

And please don't leave those tax coupons on the kitchen table unused!

LESSON 5

Free Minds and Free Markets Create Wealth

Mother at Christmas time

The Little Red Hen

*"The problem with socialism is that you
eventually run out of other people's money."*
Margaret Thatcher, Prime Minister of England 1979 - 1990

Mother found this version of *The Little Red Hen* in an old
Readers Digest and read it to us a number of times.

*One summer day, the Little Red Hen found some grains of
wheat. She called her neighbors and said, "If we plant this wheat,
we shall have bread to eat. Who will help me plant it?"*

"Not I," said the cow.

"Not I," said the duck.

"Not I," said the pig.

"Not I," said the goose.

*"Then I will plant it myself," said the Little Red Hen. And she
did. Soon the wheat grew tall and ripened into golden grain.*

"Who will help me reap the wheat?" asked the Little Red Hen.

"Not I," said the Duck.

"Out of my classification," said the pig.

"I'd lose my seniority," said the cow.

"I'd lose my unemployment compensation," said the goose.

"Then I will reap it myself," said the Little Red Hen. And she did. She reaped the wheat and had it ground into flour.

At last it was time to bake the bread. "Who will help me bake the bread?" asked the Little Red Hen.

"That would be overtime for me," said the cow.

"I'd lose my welfare benefits," said the duck.

"I'm a dropout and never learned how," said the pig.

"If I'm to be the only helper, that's discrimination," said the goose.

"Then I will," said the Little Red Hen. She baked five loaves of bread and held them up for her neighbors to see. All the barnyard animals wanted to eat some of the bread; in fact, they demanded a share. But the Little Red Hen said, "No, I made the bread myself and my children and I can eat it all."

"Excess profits!" yelled the cow.

"Capitalist leech!" cried the duck.

"I demand equal rights!" shouted the Goose.

The pig just grunted.

Then they hurriedly painted "unfair" picket signs and marched around shouting obscenities.

The government agent came and said to the Little Red Hen, "You must share the bread with the other animals. You must not be greedy."

"But I did the work necessary to create the bread. It is my personal property," said the Little Red Hen.

"Exactly," said the government agent. "That is the wonderful economic system we live in. Anyone in the barnyard can produce as much as they want, but under government regulations the productive workers must give part of what they produce to the idle. If you don't share, we will throw you in jail."

The Little Red Hen was forced by the government to give the bread she had worked so hard to produce to the rest of the animals. And they all lived happily ever after.

But the Little Red Hen's neighbors wondered why she never baked bread again.

The Little Red Hen's actions were a direct result of the economic system she found herself living in. Your actions and success depend on the economic system you live and work in, too. There are three predominant economic systems operating in the world today. See if you can determine which one you are living and working in.

Capitalism

Capitalism, or the free enterprise system, is based on individual freedom, limited government and objective laws that protect private property rights. It is an economic system in which supply, demand, price, distribution and investments are all determined by *private individuals in the free marketplace, rather than by the government through central economic planning.* Private property rights are protected by law. Whatever you produce belongs to you and it cannot be taken from you by your neighbor or the government.

Capitalism rewards productive people, like the Little Red Hen, and penalizes people who refuse to work, like the lazy barnyard animals. Under Capitalism, the Little Red Hen would have been free to produce her bread and keep it all. The other animals in the barnyard would have no claim on her private property. *The government would have been prevented by its own objective laws from interfering with the free trade of private citizens.*

Privately owned businesses produce profits that create jobs, fund education, research, enlightenment and human progress. *Before you can have endowments, charities and social programs, someone has to be free to create a profit.* Profits belong to the owner of a business, and wages are paid to workers employed by that business. Employees are free to leave their employment at any time to find a better job.

Capitalism makes up the entire economic fabric of the American society. Although Capitalism is the dominant economic system in the United States, socialism has infected our economy over the last fifty years. Today, most Americans don't understand the difference between Capitalism and Socialism.

Socialism

Socialism is an economic system where production and trade is coordinated by the government, not private citizens. The economy is controlled by government regulations through centralized economic planning. Private individuals and businesses no longer control sales, profits, interest rates or wages. Government regulation and social programs control the marketplace, not the law of supply

> *"The problem with socialism is that you eventually run out of other people's money."*
> Margaret Thatcher,
> Prime Minister
> of England 1979 - 1990

and demand. Businesses are funded by government favor, not by consumer demand. In a socialist economy there are public-private partnerships between government and business.

There are many varieties of socialism, and they differ only in the type of social ownership they advocate and the degree to which they rely on the profits of capitalism to fund government social programs. Government control and regulation of health care, banks and financial institutions, money supply, railroads, electrical, water and sewage utilities are just a few examples of socialist programs that currently exist in the United States.

Socialism is a conspiracy of the greedy to exploit the productive members of society. Socialism is an insurance policy bought by the members of a society to shield the non-productive from the responsibility of living a productive life. Socialism enables citizens to be lazy and live off the productive ability of others. Socialists believe that wealth is something that can be seized and redistributed instead of something that has to be created. They believe that by seizing the *means* of production they can capture the *secret* of production created by an entrepreneurial mind.

Today in the United States, you find yourself like the Little Red Hen working and producing, but being forced by the government to surrender a part or all of that which you produce. Your income is redistributed in the form of government programs according to government favor or group citizenship. Who receives your hard earned money? That is determined by whichever gang is in power at the moment. In a socialist society, everyone has more right to your money than you do! They are called "the public."

Socialism is a transitional stage on the economic road to Communism.

Communism

Communism demands that all the productive energy (money, goods and services) of the group (country) is put in a communal economic pool and re-distributed to those who need it the most. Each person is to produce to his or her ability and receive government handouts according to their need. The government sets the guidelines for redistributing the wealth of the nation. Everything is owned by the government. There are no private property rights.

Communism works like a hippy commune of the 1960's, but applied to an entire country. There's a reason there are no more communes today; they don't work as an economic system. The economic collapse of Russia and the Eastern Bloc Countries, which occurred in the last half of the twentieth century proved that.

In a Communist society, there are not enough people willing to work as slaves to support the people who will not work. A communist government has to physically force its citizens to work for the benefit of others. That is called slavery. Under a system of slavery, *those who work are expected to produce for those who will not work.* Under such a system, you find yourself like the Little Red Hen – working hard to produce bread, but being forced to give it to those who will not produce. *Communism is socialism at its most extreme.*

Mother was fiercely independent and would never have considered the government a source of income. If anyone from the government had come to the farm to offer financial help, Mother would have escorted them off her property with a shotgun.

Mother understood the difference between Communism, Socialism and Capitalism. She made sure that all her children did, too. Sometimes she would give me a job, like mowing the pasture, and teach an economics lesson at the same time. When I had finished mowing the pasture, she would say, "Under

Communism, I will put the money you earned into our collective grocery budget to feed the entire family. Under Socialism, I will take part of the money for my administration and regulation of your work. You will get whatever is left over, if there is any. Under Capitalism, you will get all the money you earned, because it belongs to you by right."

Which economic system do you live and work in? Which economic system would you like to live and work in? What economic system would you like your children to grow up in?

Perhaps you should read *The Little Red Hen* to your children like my Mother did.

Blueprint for a Free Society

*We hold these truths self evident. That all men are
created equal, that they are endowed by their creator
with certain inalienable rights, among these are life,
liberty and the pursuit of happiness, that to secure these
rights governments are instituted among men.*
Thomas Jefferson, Declaration of Independence 1776

In 1920, the 19th amendment to the U.S. Constitution gave
women the right to vote. Mother was part of the first generation
of American women to have that right, and she took her civic
duty very seriously. She studied the Constitution and learned how
our government operates. She read everything she could find by
Thomas Jefferson, James Madison and the other Founding Fathers. She studied candidates and listened to what they said, and
more importantly, watched what they did.

Mother thought it was her civic duty to vote, and she exercised her voting rights every time there was an election. No matter what else was going on, she knew that her responsibility as a
citizen was to exercise her constitutional right to determine the
leadership of her city, county, state and national government.

One cold and icy November, Mother and Daddy left us at
home to go to the Eastover Community Building to vote. They
were gone for hours. Finally, Mother called to tell us that Daddy's
pickup truck had slid off the icy road into the ditch. Mother had
walked the rest of the way to Eastover to vote, and then called us
to let us know she was alright. She was not going to let a little

thing like a car in the ditch stop her from voting.

Mother worked in her community as an advocate of individual liberty and freedom. She joined the Democratic Party, but when that party changed its platform from protecting the independence and freedom of individual citizens to "tax and spend" social policies, she moved to the Republican Party. She liked to say, "I didn't leave the Democratic Party. They left me." That's a sentiment a lot of Democrats who became Republicans had, including Jesse Helms and Ronald Reagan. Over time, she became known as a powerful force in the political community.

A young, successful attorney who lived in our area wanted to run for the North Carolina House of Representatives. He talked to the local Republican Party leaders, and they told him if he wanted to be elected to the N.C. House he would need to talk to Mary Monroe. He called and made an appointment with Mother to discuss his campaign.

Years later, that attorney told me that when he went to Mother's house, sat down at her lazy-susan kitchen table with a cup of fresh brewed coffee, she explained things to him about how government functioned that he had never been taught in law school. Mother taught him what Adam Smith, a Scotsman from the 18th century, believed. A limited government was a good government if its primary functions are:
1. To raise and support an army to maintain national security and protect the citizens from foreign invaders.
2. To raise and support a police force to protect citizens from each other.

3. To support a court system based on objective laws to settle
   disputes and protect citizens from the wrongs committed
   against them by other citizens.
4. To perform functions that private citizens cannot perform.

Free men and women need rules to live by. The Declaration
of Independence and the Constitution of the United States define these rules. These two documents remain the defining statement of the American Ideal and the greatest political statement
of human liberty in the history of mankind. They address the
rights of citizens and limit the rights of government. They define
*a government whose purpose is to secure the liberty of its citi-
zens.* They define the objective laws that protect private property
rights. The best government rests on the consent of the governed.
The Founding Fathers believed in the ability of men and women
to govern themselves and they distrusted the unchecked power of
government. They knew that *government is the most dangerous
threat that exists to the freedom of citizens.*

*There is one indispensable principle when you are creating a
free society; the principle of individual rights.* A *"right"* means
freedom from physical compulsion by others or the government.
The concept of *"rights"* pertains only to freedom of action by an
individual; not a group. There is only one fundamental individual
right; the right to live your own life and make the decisions necessary to further that life without interference from others or the
government.

The *"right"* of one man, cannot violate the rights of another. If
a government decides that some men are entitled to the products

of the work of others by *right*, it means that those others are condemned to slave labor. There can be no such thing as *"the right to enslave."*

If you want to determine the modern day relationship of individual freedom to the goals of today's intellectuals and political leaders, simply look at how they handle the concept of individual rights. Most political leaders evade, distort and seldom discuss *individual* freedom.

If you want to uphold and protect individual rights then the free society in the United States is the system that achieved it. That is what Thomas Jefferson meant when he wrote in the Declaration of Independence:

We hold these truths self evident. That all men are created equal, that they are endowed by their creator with certain inalienable rights, among these are life, liberty and the pursuit of happiness, that to secure these rights governments are instituted among men.

Notice that Jefferson spoke of the right to *life,* which means that a man has the right to do whatever is necessary to support his own life. It does not mean that others are required to provide him with the necessities of life.

The right to own property does not mean that others are supposed to provide you with property. He spoke of the right to liberty, which means that each individual citizen has the right to run his or her life the way that benefits them the most.

Jefferson spoke of the right to the *pursuit of happiness,* not the right to happiness itself. That means that a free citizen has the right to take any actions he deems necessary to achieve his own happiness. It does not mean that others are supposed to make him happy.

The right to *free speech* means that you have the right to express your ideas without danger of suppression, interference or punitive action by the government. It does not mean that others must provide you with a platform to express those ideas.

We hold these truths self evident. That all men are created equal, that they are endowed by their creator with certain inalienable rights, among these are life, liberty and the pursuit of happiness, that to secure these rights governments are instituted among men.
Thomas Jefferson,
Declaration of Independence, 1776

The United States government derives its powers from the consent of the governed and that is you. The Constitution of the United States was not written to tell you what to do; it was written to tell the government what it may or may not do. You do not belong to the government; the government belongs to you. The government does not empower you; you empower the government. Government is of the people.

If you own a business, you hire the very best employees you can find. If you own a house, you hire the very best workers you can find to do necessary repairs. If your child is sick, you hire the very best physician you can find to help them.

America is your business, house and child. You should hire only the very best people to look after it for you. You have a responsibility to pick the right people regardless of their party, race or gender. You have a responsibility to choose people for their talent and integrity to run your government.

Researching the candidates and voting is your civic duty. Listen to what the candidates say, and more importantly, what they do. Learn what they stand for and ask yourself, does it make sense? When you vote, you are choosing employees for your government, not masters of your life. You are choosing servants of your will and the guardians of your rights. You must demand the very best from your government.

Mother would remind you that voting is a privilege that women did not get until 1920. Get out and vote. It is what free people do. It is what people around the world who do not have the right to vote, wish they could do. Make sure you exercise your privilege and vote, even if your truck slips off an icy road into the ditch. Mother would not let an icy road stop her from voting and neither should you.

A Ticket and Two Flat Tires

*"The most important single central fact about a free market is
that no exchange takes place unless both parties benefit."*
Milton Friedman

Mother loved to visit Thigpen's Antiques near Jacksonville,
NC. She enjoyed walking among the old chairs and tables trying
to find treasures hidden in that dusty old barn. She loved primi-
tive antiques, and over the years, learned to recognize the really
valuable pieces. She learned how to take an old painted or dam-
aged piece of furniture and refinish it into a beautiful antique
that would last a hundred years. To me it was just a bunch of old
furniture that hurt your backside when you sat on it.

Usually Mother's shopping trips to Thigpens involved just her
and my sister Mary, but today Mother wanted me to drive her to
Thigpens. It was definitely not what a 16 year old boy wanted to
do on a great summer day. Apparently Thigpen had called to say
he had some fabulous antiques that Mother would be interested
in. She wanted me to drive so I could load her purchases into the
car and nothing I said would put her off.

With Mother as my passenger, I drove her blue Ford LTD
to Clinton and turned right onto Highway 24, heading toward
Thigpen's Antiques. Highway 24 is a four lane divided highway
with a grass median. After a few miles, I passed a State Patrol
cruiser headed in the opposite direction. As soon as I passed him,
he turned on his blue lights, did a quick U-turn across the grassy
median and raced up behind me with his siren on. I was definitely

not speeding, because Mother was in the car, so I did not understand why I was being pulled over.

It didn't take long for the officer to explain that the safety inspection sticker on Mother's car was out of date. I received the first traffic ticket of my lifetime (there have been many more over the years). After a brief but forceful scolding by the State Patrolman, I was back on the road to Thigpens, so angry that I could have bitten nails in half. My life was ruined because Mother had forced me to come on this trip, failed to inspect her car on time, and it was all her fault! Oh my goodness, I was angry.

Mother said she would pay for my ticket, but nothing she said could make me feel better. When we arrived at Thigpens, she went inside to shop, but I stayed in the yard fuming and fussing. She was in there buying junk, and she didn't care that my life was ruined forever. If I could have calmed down and examined the situation with a clear mind, it might have been an interesting day, but that was beyond my capabilities at sixteen years old.

Sometimes life is like my day going to Thigpens. If we could just calm down and examine the situation with a clear mind, we could find a lesson in every day. Take Thigpen's Antiques, for example. Walking through Thigpen's barn was walking through a living example of the Free Enterprise System or Capitalism. The endless variety of furniture that Thigpen had in his place was amazing. Thigpen bought furniture hoping to resell it for a higher price and make a profit. Mother hoped to buy a piece of furniture cheap and, with some tender loving care, turn it into something much more valuable. Each of them wanted to benefit from the exchange.

Thigpen offered his very best products at the very best price he could. His success was based upon how well he satisfied his consumer's needs. If he stocked things that his customers wanted, he was successful. If he offered things that nobody wanted or at too high of a price, then he would fail. The opinion of the customers was what determined the success or failure of his business.

Mother got to pick and choose the best value for herself. The person who benefits most from the free market (capitalism) is the consumer. The free market works because the consumer always gets the best products at the best value. Capitalism is characterized by private individuals making decisions and acting in their own personal best interest. That is how a free market works. Everybody wins because *no exchange takes place unless both parties benefit.*

One of the books that Mother made me read was Milton Friedman's Nobel Prize winning book, *Capitalism and Freedom.* She told me that everyone was required to read it in high school.

Capitalism and Freedom was originally published in 1962, and has been translated into eighteen languages. It explains why individual freedom and private property rights are a requirement for any society to prosper. Friedman makes the case for economic freedom as a precondition for political freedom. He uses concrete evidence to show that large federal government spending makes the economy less stable.

Here is what Freidman says about the free market: *"The only way that has ever been discovered to have a lot of people cooperate together voluntarily is through the free market. And that's why it's so essential to preserving individual freedom. Most good things in the United States and the world come from the free market, not the government, and they will continue to do so. The government, despite its good intentions, should stay out of private enterprise."*

In a free market, a business cannot force their customer to purchase their products or service. *Only the government can force private citizens to purchase one product or service over another.* In the United States today, government created and controlled monopolies exist all around us. Government control and regulation of health care, banks and financial institutions, money supply, railroads, electrical, water and sewage utilities are just a few examples of socialist programs that currently exist. To paraphrase Friedman, the government should stay out of private business.

A few years ago, I was speaking on Capitalism in Raleigh, N.C. and on one of the breaks an attendee from Nassau, The Bahamas said to me,

"It is interesting to watch the government of United States operate from The Bahamas. I am struck by the fact that your country operates two different economic systems at the same time. You are a capitalist government for individuals and a socialist government for large industry. We watch your country give billions of dollars to railroads, airlines, banking and auto manufactures, and yet allow individual small business to fail by the thousands!

"The more disturbing trend is to watch your government restrict and destroy the chance of economic survival of individuals and small businesses with their local, state and national laws. Watching from The Bahamas, we find it all very confusing."

On my day driving to Thigpens, I could have learned a lot about the free enterprise system if I had not been so upset with my ticket. After stewing in the parking lot and wandering around in that dusty old barn, I finally calmed down. Mother paid Thigpen for her purchases and I loaded them into the car. We headed home. When we approached the spot in the road where I got my ticket, there was a loud bang, and the car suddenly lurched to the right. I had a flat tire. I pulled onto the shoulder of the road and began the hot, dirty task of changing the tire. Then I discovered that to access the spare tire, I had to unload all of the furniture from the trunk!

> *"The most important single central fact about a free market is that no exchange takes place unless both parties benefit."*
> Milton Friedman

Back on the road I was hot, sweaty, dirty and angry again. Could this day get any worse? Yes it could.

About a mile from home the spare tire blew out. We now had two flat tires and no spare. Mother told me to drive home on the flat tire. I didn't argue; I just wanted this day to be over. I continued to drive with the tire making a whump, whump, whumping noise as we went slowly down Middle Road. Finally, and thankfully, we arrived home with a ticket, two flat tires and a bunch of old furniture. I am not sure the trip was worth the effort.

My trip to Thigpens was a disaster by any account. A ticket and two flat tires would qualify as a bad day in anyone's book. I did not learn the lesson on the free enterprise system that was available that day until years later.

Perhaps you should visit Thigpens to get a quick lesson on how a free market works. Perhaps you should take your children with you and turn your trip into a lesson on Free Market Capitalism.

Just make sure you inspect the family car first!

A Gardener Needs Seeds

"A seed contains all the ingredients necessary for life."
Mary Monroe

In the middle of the winter, Mother could be found sitting in her big red chair reading seed catalogues. She would pour over the pages trying to decide which seeds she wanted to order for spring. Then she would fill out the order form with her cursive writing and wait impatiently until her seeds arrived.

She would keep the seeds in her kitchen cabinet over the winter so they would remain dormant in the dark. In the spring she would bring them out to begin the germination process. She would soak the seeds in water overnight and then lay them on a wet paper towel in the warm sunshine on her front porch. Once the seeds began to swell and sprout, she would gently plant them in an ice cube tray with a little bit of rich black earth. Soon their little leaves would appear, and she would know they had taken root. Once they were strong enough, she would carefully transfer them to a small pot to grow. Finally, the little plants would be transplanted into the garden to begin life on their own in the great big world.

Mother would say, "A seed contains all the ingredients necessary for life, but they will not grow unless they are nurtured by the gardener under the right conditions. There are consequences to being a gardener, both good and bad. Place your seeds in the right environment and cultivate them, and you will be successful. Plant your seeds in the wrong environment or fail to cultivate them, and you will fail."

Money is just like a seed. Money contains all the ingredients necessary to grow wealth. Money left idle is just like a seed kept in the dark; it cannot possibly sprout and grow. Wealth will never sprout and grow on its own; you must cultivate it.

If you eat your seeds you will not have anything to plant in the spring. If you spend your money, you will have nothing to invest. Money will not teach you how to generate wealth any more than a seed will teach you how to grow a tree. Just like seeds, money must be planted in the right environment to grow. Creating wealth is just like growing a garden; it bears consequences.

A Capitalist needs money just like a gardener needs seeds. A gardener has a right to the fruits and vegetables of their garden because they created it. It is their property. An Entrepreneur has a right to their profits because they create them. It is their property. It makes no more sense to begrudge the entrepreneur his profits than to begrudge the gardener her seeds. Capitalists need capital to launch and finance their business enterprise. The reason capitalism works is that the creators of wealth are guaranteed the right and responsibility of reinvesting their profits. The creators of wealth are captives of their money. They can keep it only to the extent that they replant the seeds of wealth into another business venture.

> *"A seed contains all the ingredients necessary for life"*
> Mary Monroe

Mother knew how to plant the seeds of wealth. She was part

owner of Kings Shopping Center on Bragg Boulevard in Fayetteville. The owner of the property next door wanted to purchase an unused strip of land between the shopping center and his property. Mother sold that strip of land and planted that seed money into the purchase of a house that she rented to generate income. The fruits of that seed money continue to produce rental income for our family today. Trading a piece of land that was not producing any return for a rental house that was an income producing asset is an example of germinating the seeds of wealth.

You need seeds to plant your garden. You need seed money to plant your investments. Without seeds, you cannot grow a garden, and without money to invest, you cannot grow wealth. Spend less than you earn and plant the rest in your financial garden. Money contains all the ingredients necessary to create wealth, but it will not plant itself.

Food Tastes Better at Honey's House

"It doesn't matter how much money you take in;
it matters what you spend."
Mary Monroe

My children were always hungry when we visited Mother's house. I could feed them before we left home, but as soon as we arrived at her house they would beg for food like they had not eaten in weeks. There was something about the way her house smelled that made them hungry. I have to admit I always wanted to eat at her house, too. It was her fried chicken, mashed potatoes and butter beans that they wanted. My personal favorite was her fresh baked sesame seed rolls with sweet creamy butter and homemade blackberry jelly.

Sitting at Mother's table watching my children wolf down her food was a great time for Mother and me to talk. I had achieved a fairly high level of success in the real estate business, managing a large company and living in a big house with all the trimmings. I had a successful lifestyle to go along with my new found financial success. To put it simply, I was making more money than I had ever made in my life and I was spending it. I wasn't saving any money. I was spending all my income paying for the things I had bought on credit.

"Why does it take you so much money to live?" Mother asked.

"Because I have car payments, house payments, boat payments and credit card payments," I replied.

"But why does it take you so much money to live?" Mother asked again.

"Because I have car payments, house payments, boat payments and credit card payments," I replied a little exasperated.

"Exactly!" Mother exclaimed. "If you would live within your means, not spending money you don't have, then you would not be in this mess. If you had the self-discipline to *spend less than you earn,* you would be financially sound. You are acting just like the government; spending money you don't have and expecting somehow, someday it will be okay. You cannot fake reality. You cannot spend money you don't have and neither can the government. You cannot have your cake and eat it too. You cannot spend your way to prosperity. You will end up just like the government, broke and bankrupt! There has to be a day of reckoning when you must tighten your belt, spend less than you earn and do without those things you cannot afford. *It doesn't matter how much money you take in; it matters what you spend.*"

Mother had a way with words, and when she got worked up on a subject like debt, you just had to sit there and take it. After I got over being angry with Mother for telling me the truth, I realized that she was right. Neither I, nor the government, can spend money that we don't have.

A nation's economy is just like your household budget. A government cannot spend money it doesn't have. For the last fifty years the United States Government has spent more money than it has taken in. Every year the U.S. government spends one dollar for every seventy-five cents it receives in taxes. As of June, 2015, the United States federal debt has reached almost eighteen trillion point two. According to the May/June 2015 Cato Policy Report, *Running Out of Other People's Money* by Michael Tanner:

Let's put that (eighteen trillion point two) into perspective: The Los Angeles Dodgers have the biggest payroll in baseball. For eighteen trillion point two, *you could pay the Dodgers for sixty-five thousand, two hundred and four years, and still have money left over for a couple of free-agent pitchers. And, speaking of Los Angeles,* eighteen trillion point two *could buy all the real estate in LA thirty eight times over. If we were to pay our national debt back at the rate of one dollar per second, we could wipe it out in a mere five hundred seventy-six thousand, seven hundred thirty-six years. Each American's share of that debt is more than fifty-six thousand, seven hundred fifty dollars.*

As citizens, we will have to come to terms with our government's debt. We cannot continue to spend money that we don't have and pay no attention to the consequences. We are fast approaching a day of reckoning when the government will have to tighten their belts, spend less than they take in on taxes and do without some things they cannot afford. If we do not, we will not survive financially as a country.

Will we, as a country, learn to curtail our spending, tighten our belts and do without some things until we get our debt paid off? I doubt it. I think as a country we will continue acting like a spoiled child, spending money we don't have and blaming someone else. We will have to learn as a country, as I did, that you cannot spend money you don't have.

After Mother's scolding at her kitchen table, I continued to spend money I didn't have for a few years. One day I woke up to find myself deep in debt. It took me years to dig my way out of that debt and work my way back to being financially sound. Finally, when I had paid off every last cent, I learned Mother's lesson, *"It doesn't matter how much money you take in; it matters what you spend."*

> *"It doesn't matter how much money you take in; it matters what you spend."*
> Mary Monroe

Today, I wish I could take my children back to Mother's house for one more meal. We could sit there and enjoy the sesame seed rolls, butter and homemade blackberry jelly. My children could hear their grandmother tell them that it doesn't matter how much money they made in life; it matters how much they spend. They could learn that they could only spend less than they earned and invest the rest.

Perhaps if the government could come to Honey's house and get a good scolding, they would learn the lesson she tried to teach me. The elected officials that we have running our country could learn how to get government spending under control. Perhaps they would learn that a government is no different from a single household when it comes to money. You cannot spend more than you take in.

Mother is no longer with us, so I guess it is up to you and me to tell our government to get off this *"tax and spend cycle"* that is bankrupting our country. I think you better get ready for this meeting. Mother would recommend fried chicken, mashed potatoes and butterbeans. For dessert she would have sesame seed rolls, butter and homemade blackberry jelly.

151

You Might be a Redneck Capitalist

"Play with a puppy and he will lick you in the face."
Mary Monroe

Mother loved the humor of Jeff Foxworthy. She would sit by her television and laugh at his famous comedy routine, *You Might be a Redneck.* Here is an example Jeff Foxworthy's humor:

- You might be a redneck if... you ever cut your grass and found a car.
- You might be a redneck if... you own a home that is mobile and 5 cars that aren't.
- You might be a redneck if... you think the stock market has a fence around it.
- You might be a redneck if... your stereo speakers used to belong to the Drive-in Theater.
- You might be a redneck if... your boat has not left your driveway in 15 years.
- You might be a redneck if... your mother has "ammo" on her Christmas list.
- You might be a redneck if... the Home Shopping operator recognizes your voice.
- You might be a redneck if... the taillight covers of your car are made of red tape.
- You might be a redneck if... you have ever spray-painted your girlfriend's name on an overpass.
- You might be a redneck if... people hear your car a long time before they see it.
- You might be a redneck if... you've ever been involved in a custody fight over a hunting dog.

152

Jeff Foxworthy makes us laugh because his humor is about real life in America. We would all like to think that we are sophisticated, but lots of us have discovered that we are actually rednecks.

What if you discovered you actually were a redneck? How would it change your life? Would you change your personal perception of how you function in society?

What if you discovered you were actually a Capitalist? Would you change your perception of what Capitalism is? Would it change your life to know you live in a Capitalist society?

My Mother would say:
- You might be a Capitalist if... you ever quit a job of your own free will to take a better job.
- You might be a Capitalist if... you are working in a career you chose instead of having the government choose one for you.
- You might be a Capitalist if... you put money into a savings account.
- You might be a Capitalist if... you have money invested in a tax sheltered Profit Sharing Plan or Individual Retirement Account (IRA).
- You might be a Capitalist if... you ever had an idea that made you money.
- You might be a Capitalist if... you worked to pay off the mortgage on your house (1/3 of all houses in the United States are paid for free and clear).
- You might be a Capitalist if... you ever started a business.
- You might be a Capitalist if... you believe in private property rights.

- You might be a Capitalist if... you believe that wealth is created by free minds and free markets.
- You might be a Capitalist if... you believe in free trade among private citizens.
- You might be a Capitalist if... you think people should run their own lives without interference from the government.
- You might be a Capitalist if... you believe that private business can do a better job of providing goods and services to you than the government.
- You might be a Capitalist if... you made a career by making people laugh like Jeff Foxworthy!

The United States is not successful because we have a big government, big business or a big military. The United States is successful because we are a society of people who think and act like Capitalists. We create small, privately owned businesses that produce the wealth of our nation. Free minds and free markets have created more prosperity and wealth for the people of the world than any other economic system in history.

However, Capitalism is the most maligned and misunderstood economic system in the world. In my research for this book, I searched the internet for images of capitalism. *Of the 41 million images that were produced, I did not find any positive images of capitalism.* Every image was of oppression, control and destruction. How can the world misunderstand an economic system that is based upon individual freedom, private property rights and free trade for mutual

"Play with a puppy and he will lick you in the face."
Mary Monroe

benefit? How can the entire world misunderstand a system that has created the greatest prosperity the world has ever known?

Thank you, Jeff Foxworthy, for making my mother laugh and changing the way we look at the American society. Thanks to my mother for changing the way our family looked at Capitalism.

Take the time to learn more about free market Capitalism and you might discover you are a *Redneck Capitalist* like me!

Free Minds and Free Markets Create Wealth

"Free minds and free markets create wealth."
Mary Monroe

Behind the horse barn there were some old timbers left over from one of Mother's construction projects. One cold November day, she asked me to split those timbers to make a rail fence. I went to the tool shed, got an ax and sharpened it, but before I could begin, my best friend G. L. Draughon stopped by. He wanted me to ride around in his car, as teenagers like to do. I told him I had to work for Mother splitting the timbers to make a fence. I am sure he made some comment about my lack of skill with an ax.

Well, his comments were all I needed to prove him wrong. With G.L. heckling me, I marched him out behind the barn, rolled one of the timbers away from the others and sunk my ax deep into one end, working my way up the center to the other end. I was feeling a lot like Abraham Lincoln at this point. In just a few minutes, the timber cracked open and revealed a center of hard, yellow pine.

Both of us realized that this timber might look old and rotten on the outside, but inside it was heart pine. The center of an old growth pine tree will solidify into a hard yellow resin we call "heart pine or fat lighter." It smells like a fresh cut Christmas tree. If you leave fat lighter in the sun shine, the resin will begin to liquefy and ooze. That resin is nature's gasoline. All you have to do is touch it with a match and it will catch fire. My Uncle Don used to joke that, if you left a piece of fat lighter in the sunshine on a hot day, it would catch fire.

G.L. and I realized we didn't just have a pile of timbers to split, but a pile of heart pine, fat lighter logs. We knew that people would pay for fat lighter because it was very difficult to find. We ran to the house and told Mother, "These timbers are actually heart pine fat lighter logs and we don't think the best use for them would be a split rail fence."

She agreed and asked, "What do you have in mind?"

"We could split the timbers up into small pieces, bundle them together and sell them as kindling."

Mother agreed, and my first business partnership was formed right there behind the horse barn. I remember Mother watching us create our little business with a smile on her face. Now I know she we encouraging me to become an entrepreneur.

G.L.'s family owned a meat packing business and a chain of grocery stores. We agreed that if I cut the timbers into small bundles, G.L. would buy them from me for one dollar each, then resell the kindling in his stores. G.L. left and I began to split the timbers into smaller and smaller pieces. Mother brought me some baling twine, and I bound them together into six inch thick packets and stacked them in the yard. Each packet was worth one dollar.

When I was working for Mother I had no interest in splitting the rails. Now that it was my own business, the work became fun. I was seeing dollar signs with each swing of my ax. I could see my money grow as my pile of kindling grew. I was happy to work until dark because now, I was working for myself, not someone else. I realized that, when you own your own business, you become much more productive.

By the time it was too dark to see, I had fifty packets of kindling ready for sale. G.L. came by the next day, paid me fifty dollars and took those bundles to one of his grocery stores. He priced each bundle at two dollars each and doubled his investment. That is when I learned the difference between wholesale and retail. I was selling the bundles in bulk at wholesale prices and G.L. was retailing the bundles for twice as much money in his grocery store. He did not have the timbers to split, and I did not have a grocery store to sell kindling in. Together we both made money. That is how a partnership works.

G.L. called me a few days later to say all of the bundles were sold and he was ready for more. Our new business was underway, fueled by the energy of two young entrepreneurs, a product consumers wanted and the right distribution channel. Free minds and free markets create wealth. G.L. and I chose to start our business without any promise of success. We took the chance based on our knowledge of what others needed and our belief that our product would add value to their lives.

Mother taught us that productive work is the purpose of life. G.L. and I never minded doing work that others did not deem worthy of them. Profit all too often comes from doing what other people consider beneath them. Wealth is not created by knowing what the experts know, but by doing something with the knowledge that other people value. Entrepreneurship is the launching of new products and services that add value to the lives of the customers. A successful entrepreneur pays close attention to the wants and needs of their consumer.

Our kindling business could have failed if we delivered a product to the market that no one wanted or charged too high a price. If we tried to sell kindling in the middle of July, our customers would not have needed our product.

Entrepreneurship is about taking a chance and gaining a reward. The reward for our idea, risk, time and efforts was the profit. *Profit is the result of a great idea applied in a free market.* Profit was the driving force of our small business. G.L. and I were not interested in working and risking our time and money without making a profit. To ask someone to take action and not profit from those actions is insanity. *No animal on earth would act in a manner that would not enhance their own lives.* Yet today, society tells us that everyone should work for the public good instead of themselves. We were not motivated by helping our fellow man build a fire. We were motivated by helping ourselves. The ultimate strength of capitalism is the reliance on individual ideas, actions and profits from those actions.

> *"Free minds and free markets create wealth."*
> Mary Monroe

Profit is the byproduct of creating a valuable product or service in a free market. A product or service is valuable only if combined with knowledge and action. Rotting timbers were not valuable to anyone as long as they were left behind the horse barn. They only became valuable when the minds of two young entrepreneurs saw their potential for another use.

Profit is an indicator of the value of product or service. Profit is the difference between the cost of an item to the business and its value to the customer. Most of the people who bought our little packets of fat lighter probably owned an ax. It was worth two dollars per packet not to have to go find the fat lighter logs in the woods and cut their own kindling.

Free markets grow because they award profits to entrepreneurs who have already proved that they can reinvest that money. A successful entrepreneur does not consume his income; he faces the challenge and responsibility of reinvesting his profits. Capitalism succeeds because it assigns this exacting task to people who have proven they know what to do with the money. I took the money I made that year selling kindling and reinvested it into a chain saw. I found that very few of our neighbors had a chain saw, so there was an opportunity for me to provide a service and earn some money. I used that chain saw to cut down trees for Mother and other people in the neighborhood to make money. Later on I discovered that the chain saw did not like me, so I sold it to Uncle Don, but that is a story for another time.

Free minds and free markets create wealth. People should be free of government constraints to create, act and profit in their own best interest. Creativity cannot be planned or demanded by government. Governmental intervention into a free economy nearly always retards entrepreneurial ideas. You cannot have a more efficient economy by suppressing entrepreneurial spirit with government power.

The process of entrepreneurship is offensive to socialists because it yields mountains of new wealth in ways that could not possibly have been planned. No government agency could have predicted the consumer needs of our kindling. Only the minds of young entrepreneurs, who did all this work to put gas in our cars, was the driving force of our business.

All economic progress comes from the mind of an entrepreneur. An entrepreneur's value is their experience and knowledge put into action. Our business was born in our minds first and then turned into profit when we took action. If we had been lazy or the government had put money into our empty wallets, we would have wasted the afternoon instead of starting a business. I could have gone back into the house and watched television and made no money. I didn't have to split the timbers, but entrepreneurs are willing to focus on the needs of others to create a profit.

Our little business continued all winter that year until the warm spring ended our chance to sell kindling. I worked day after day to keep G.L. supplied with kindling, and he worked tirelessly to get them sold. I remember Mother watching us with a smile as I traded my kindling for money under the carport that winter. She was proud that together G.L and I made good money and learned a great lesson too.

Free minds and free markets create wealth.

LESSON 6

Profit is Better Than Wages

Honey on her front porch
1991

Profit is Better than Wages

"Profit is better than wages."
Mary Monroe

A hundred years ago everyone was in business. We were the butcher, the baker, the candlestick maker. We were farmers, carpenters, cooks and store owners. We did whatever was necessary to earn a living.

Today, we teach our children to go to school, get a good education, and then "get a good job." The problem with a job is that it never teaches you how to run a business. School doesn't teach you how to be a success. You have to learn that on your own.

When I was sixteen, Mother said I had to get a summer job. I had worked on our farm as a child, but never held a job in the public. I called my friend, Kenny Norris, whose father owned Fayetteville Wholesale Building Supply, and asked, "Do you think your dad would hire me to work in his lumberyard?"

I remember being scared to death climbing the stairs to Mr. Norris's office and standing in front of his desk. I asked him for a job, and he said, "I'll hire you. Kenny, take him out in the warehouse and show him what he'll be doing all summer."

The job they had for me in the warehouse was cutting studs. There were two men standing beside a saw, knee-deep in sawdust. They had a stack of two-by-fours on one side of the saw and another stack on the other side. They removed two pieces of lumber from one stack, put them on the saw, cut them the proper length and then stacked the cut lumber in the second pile. They were wearing goggles because there's so much sawdust and headphones because the saw was so loud. They were knee deep in sawdust because they had not moved in a long time. I wanted to drive the delivery trucks.

I went home and told Mother that a job in a warehouse wearing goggles and headphones, was not for me. She replied, "So, why don't you open your own business? Profit is better than wages."

My sister Liz suggested I open a swimming and tennis business on our farm. Our father built a tennis court when I was six years old, and Mother had a swimming pool built after he died. By the time I was sixteen, I was an excellent tennis player and swimmer. I decided to open a back yard business inviting the neighborhood kids to swim for $.50 cents per hour. I figured that teaching swimming and tennis in my back yard would be a much better summer job than working in a hot warehouse, knee deep in saw dust.

I contacted the YMCA and enrolled in Senior Life Saving and Water Safety Instructor courses so I would be certified to teach swimming, as well as lifeguard. I went to Spillman's Speedi-Print and had five hundred flyers printed advertising my backyard business. I called myself Alexander Monroe, because I thought that would make me sound like I was older and knew what I was doing. I got a few of the neighborhood kids to help me put the flyers on everyone's door in the local community. Then I waited for the business to flow in.

Sure enough, the next day children came from the surrounding community on their bikes carrying a one-dollar bill, ready to swim in my pool. Soon the pool was packed every afternoon with kids. I taught swimming classes in the morning and lifeguarded in the afternoon.

They paid fifty cents per hour to swim in my pool and I could put twenty children in the pool at the same time. I was making ten dollars an hour lifeguarding, when the lumberyard paid three dollars. Mother made me pay the electric bill for the pool and purchase all the chemicals. I was running a business at sixteen years old!

I learned how to run a business right there in my back yard. I kept my money in a zippered bank bag. If someone brought me a dollar, it went in the bag. If I had to buy chlorine, I paid for it out of the bag. The money that remained in the bag was profit. I learned about income, expenses, profit and loss and employees. I hired a girl to help me teach swimming during the summer. The fact that that she looked great in a bikini was secondary.

> *"Profit is better than wages."*
> Mary Monroe

I spent that summer in my bathing suit in my backyard and earned the same amount of money that I would have earned working at the lumberyard. The next year my income doubled. The next year it doubled again. The next year it doubled again. Mother was right. *Profit is better than wages.*

Every year, my little backyard business grew. After college I opened Cloverfield Tennis and Swim Club, Inc. with my brother-in-law. It had six tennis courts and an Olympic-sized swimming pool. I operated Cloverfield Tennis and Swim Club for the next ten years, acting as the general manager, swim instructor and U.S.P.T.A Tennis Professional. Those ten years taught me more about running a business than I would have ever learned in business school.

An entrepreneur is someone who finds a problem and creates a solution that produces a profit. I started my first business in my backyard with an idea. In any business, you should to start with your current assets, your current skills, your current abilities. If you study people who have had great success, they almost always started right where they were, satisfying the needs of others.

Before you start a business, there are some questions you should ask:

1. How will you define your market?
   - Who are your customers?
   - How will you contact them?
   - What do they need?
   - What can you help them accomplish?
   - What is the demographic profile of the people who will purchase your product or service?
   - Who will you compete with for your customer's attention?

2. What do you specialize in?
   - What is your expertise?
   - What do you know better than anyone else?
   - What can you do better than anyone else?

- What makes you unique?
- Are you known for a skill or product?
- How are you going to deliver your product or service to your customers?

3. How will you market your product or service?
   - What key words describe you and your specialized business, quickly and sharply?
   - What are you going to do to engage and capture your customers?

Today I am a speaker, teacher and consultant, but I am running the same business I ran in my backyard, years ago. I teach business classes instead of swimming lessons. I teach camps for entrepreneurs instead of tennis camps. I work with professional business people instead of working with professional tennis players. Setting up a speaking engagement is just like creating a class for swimming lessons. I simply teach business owners what I learned running my backyard tennis and swim business.

I often wonder how my life would have been different if I had taken that job in the lumber yard that summer. I would have not started my own business at sixteen and would not have learned about running a business. I would certainly not be sitting on an airplane writing this book, flying from Atlanta to Los Angeles to speak at a huge corporate event for entrepreneurs.

What assets do you have? What can you use that is right in your backyard to start your own business? What would your life be like if you took the chance and opened your own business? Take that chance and see where it will lead you.

Mother was right; *profit is better than wages.*

The Daylily Business

*"Business owners are not ordinary people
doing extraordinary things; they are extraordinary
people doing the impossible."*
Zan Monroe

Mother liked plants of all kinds so she turned her passion for growing things into a business. She was known for helping people landscape their lawns, so selling plants became a natural business for her.

Every summer, Mother ran an ad in the local newspaper advertising her daylilies, butterfly bushes, foxgloves, iris lilies, ivy, lamb's ears, summer phlox, blue phlox, autumn joy sedum, and crape myrtles for sale. Mother was known for her plants but her favorite were her many varieties of daylilies. Daylilies bloom in June in North Carolina, and their bulbs multiply themselves each year. Mother would divide her daylilies in the fall, resulting in two or three times as many as she had the year before.

When folks would come to her house to purchase plants, she would greet her customers on the front lawn and escort them to her garden. In her garden, they viewed her stunning plants in full bloom, growing in fabulous soil and in the perfect location.

Her customers would say, "I just need to get a couple of daylilies for my flower bed."

Mother would take out the plastic grocery bags she saved and dig up the plants they wanted. She did not allow anyone to dig their own daylilies because she did not want them to harm her plants. After she dug the two or three daylilies they asked for, Mother would ask, "How big of an area are you covering?"

"Oh, our garden is twenty feet long," they would say.

"Well, these two or three plants won't do it," she would tell them. "You are going to need ten or fifteen plants to go across the back of this plot just to give some basic coverage."

"How deep is your garden?" she would ask.

They would say, "It's six feet deep," and Mother would reply, "Now, to show the daylilies properly you'll need two different colors and two different kinds to coordinate and complement each other. You will need some tall ones to stand in the back and give height and the shorter ones in the front for lots of color. When you arrange your plot correctly with the right combination of daylilies, it will give you the beauty you're looking for."

Her customers would say, "Well, when you explain it like that, we need a lot more daylilies."

They would buy twenty or thirty daylilies instead of two or three and drive away satisfied and happy. Mother would tuck her money in her pocket and head back to the house. She wasn't just selling flowers to her customers, she truly wanted their gardens to look better.

Watching Mother and her daylily business, I realized one of the cardinal rules of running a successful business is to know your product. Product knowledge is more than just knowing everything you possibly can about your product or service. It is sharing that knowledge with your customers.

Mother knew the best way to care for daylilies. When people came to buy daylilies, it was simple for Mother to help them determine how many daylilies

"Business owners are not ordinary people doing extraordinary things; they are extraordinary people doing the impossible."
Zan Monroe

they needed, analyze the soil they would be planting in, and recommend care for the plants in their yard. She would give her customers a sheet of instructions that explained the life cycle, care and feeding of the daylilies. Her customers went home with much more knowledge than they expected.

Mother's business had satisfied customers who returned year after year to purchase plants. Mother could advertise and attract new customers like any other business, but she cultivated her repeat business because of her knowledge of gardening and the trust she developed with everyone. She knew it is much cheaper to keep a current customer than it is to generate a new one. Actually, my research over the years show it is six times more expensive to generate a new customer than it is to keep your current customers.

During the year, people would call her and say, "Is it time to divide my daylilies or should I fertilize them now?" She would take all the time necessary to teach them how to care for their plants. She added value to her customers by providing knowledge from her lifetime of learning.

Her repeat customers would call in the early spring and say, "When your daylilies bloom, call me. I want to be the first to select my flowers." Before Mother ran her newspaper ad she would call her preferred customers to give them first choice of the best flowers. People would place orders for the next year, saying, "Next year I'm going to want ten more of this color." The longer she ran her business, the more business came from repeat and referral customers.

It takes time to build a business, just like it takes time to grow daylilies. Every business has a gestation period, just like a plant. It takes one hundred to two hundred days to grow daylilies. It takes one hundred years to grow an oak tree. The two are completely different. The first summer that Mother ran her business, only a few people came. After a couple of years, her customer base grew through word-of-mouth marketing. Give your business time to grow. Nothing happens overnight.

People came to see Mother for more than just flowers; they could buy flowers anywhere. They were buying her expertise. They were buying her guarantee that if they had more questions, they could call her, the expert. What they were seeking was the customer experience of meeting Mother, walking in her yard and witnessing a fabulously landscaped garden. They were bonding and sharing the experience with Mother and her passion for growing things.

Today's consumer is seeking a fabulous customer experience from your business. They are buying the experience and your expertise as much as your product or service. If you provide that experience and expertise along with your product or service, then you will achieve trusted advisor status. Trusted advisor status is the highest form of customer and business bonding that exists in the marketplace today.

Trusted advisor status is not easy to achieve, but with work and focus, you can do it. Remember, *"Business owners are not ordinary people doing extraordinary things; they are extraordinary people doing the impossible."*

Taken to Jail for Playing Tennis

"A man's actions speak louder than his words."
Mary Monroe

When I was in high school, I was taken to jail for playing tennis.

Steve Dawson and I played on the high school tennis team and in the spring we would practice on the public courts at Rowan Street Park. We would start playing right after school and play until nine or ten at night. I am not sure when we did our homework.

One evening, after we finished playing, we were sitting on the hood of my car talking when Steve's girlfriend and a friend of hers, Beaufort Olive, pulled into the small parking lot. We could not let two beautiful girls play tennis all alone, so Steve and I joined them on the court. We laughed and shouted, whooped and hollered, as we played. Our noise did not matter because we were in a public park and there was no one around to hear us, or so we thought.

There was a house behind the trees, right next to the tennis courts, and the little old lady who lived there was bothered by our noise. She called the police complaining about kids making noise in the park late at night. We found out we were in trouble when the police car pulled into the parking lot and asked for our identification.

The officer asked what we were doing in the park so late.

He radioed the police station downtown that he had the "tennis playing kids from the park." Much to our surprise and his, he was told to bring us downtown to the police station. Rowan Street Park had been a hangout for hippies in the 1960's, and there was still a curfew on the park. He said the sergeant just wanted to talk to us. He took our drivers licenses so we would not escape, and we followed him in our cars to the police station. Entering the police station on the left, there was a window with bars. The officer stopped to ask what was to be done with "those tennis playing kids from Rowan Street Park?"

"Arrest them for violating the Rowan Street Park curfew!" was the answer from the police sergeant. All four of us were stunned. We were locked in a room without a phone or bathroom for the next five hours while the police tried to get a magistrate to write a warrant to have us arrested. At five o'clock the next morning, the door was unlocked and we were allowed to leave, without being arrested. Apparently the judge did not see any value in arresting tennis players in the park.

The girls were very upset because they had been out all night without their parents' permission and could not call home. Steve and I were upset, too, but relieved that we were not going to jail. I arrived home just as the sun was coming up. Mother was fixing breakfast' and when I told her what happened she said, "Well, that will teach you a lesson." She did not seem to be upset with me at all.

I headed to my bedroom to sleep, but Mother stopped me. "Oh, no, you don't. No sleep for you. You get showered and dressed and go to those girls' houses and apologize to their parents face to face. Those parents must have been scared out of their minds wondering where their daughters were. You go to their houses right now and verify their story so they will not get into any trouble. Do it now before their parents get off to work."

My morning was spent tracking down the parents of the other kids and apologizing for having their children taken to jail for playing tennis! When I finally got home, Mother said, "All you really have in life is your character and reputation. Without that, you have nothing. The reason I made you go apologize to those parents face to face is so you will remember for the rest of your life that your character and your reputation is important. *When you lead people down the wrong path you have to take personal responsibility for your actions.* When you make a mistake, like last night, you have to take personal responsibility for it. Now don't ever make a mistake like that again!"

Mother was right; *a man's actions speak louder than his words.*

Mother taught me to guard my reputation and stand by my character. Businesses must do the same thing. Your reputation is other people's opinion of you. Your character is the outward reflection of your personal values and beliefs. We all make mistakes. It is how we handle those mistakes that matter. As soon as a mistake is discovered, you must acknowledge the error, face the truth and find a way to fix it. Both your reputation and your character must be impeccable for you to be a successful person or a successful business.

Today, I am a business consultant to large companies, and I speak to tens of thousands of people each year about what it takes to make a business great. I teach them exactly what Mother taught me, "All you have is your character and reputation as a person and as a business. When you lead people down the wrong path you have to take personal responsibility for it. When you make a mistake you have to apologize and correct the error."

The successful companies that I study all have an incredible fabric of core values, underlying ideals and principles that guide them every day. The more a company is challenged, the more it must rely upon its character and reputation. Every employee in those successful companies knows the company's core values and can explain them to their customers. Great companies build their business on their reputation

> *"A man's actions speak louder than his words."*
> Mary Monroe

and character by standing behind their products and services. Customers of these great companies know that they will always be able to depend on the products and services that are backed by people of character who take responsibility for their actions. *A company's actions speak louder than their words.*

When I consult with owners and managers of companies, my advice is simple. Find people with high moral values, core beliefs and high character traits. Place them in the right spot, get out of their way and let them excel at what they love to do. Employees with integrity are the key to great companies. People of character don't have a job, they have responsibilities. They take care of their responsibilities. The right people do what they say they

179

will do because they have the right belief system. The moment you have to manage an employee's activities, you know you have hired the wrong person.

Greg Floyd is a friend of mine. I worked with him for five years while I ran his real estate, building and land development company. I watched him work every day making decisions based on his core values. He never wavered or changed those values, not even once. He held the same core beliefs and values the last time I saw him as he did the first day we met. His company built two hundred houses a year and satisfied customers' demands with excellence. He stood by his core values even when it cost him money. If he had given his word, he would honor it.

At one point he discovered that one of the houses we built was missing a foundation pier near the front door. The architect had simply forgotten to draw the pier into the blue print. We had built eleven of these houses from the faulty blue prints. All those houses were sold and occupied by the homeowners. No one had ever complained and no one would ever know about of the problem, unless we told them.

Greg knew it was a mistake his company made in building the houses and that was all that mattered. Without hesitation, he informed the homeowners and ordered his construction crews to return to all eleven houses and correct the problem. Some of the houses had been built years earlier and the second owner lived there now. It cost his company thousands of dollars to fix the problem, but he never hesitated because he runs his business based on his character and reputation. I loved working with Greg

Floyd because his character was impeccable.

A man's actions speak louder than his words.

As for my tennis career, I went on to play tennis at North Carolina State University, was ranked in the top ten tennis players in North Carolina, and played some professional tournaments. I opened Cloverfield Tennis and Swim Club at the age of 21, and was a club owner and U.S.P.T.A. Tennis professional for ten years. I have taught hundreds of people to play tennis. My tennis career was good, but my character and reputation was always more important to me than tennis. Throughout all these years, nobody ever knew that I was taken to jail for playing tennis... until now!

Mother was right; *a man's actions speak louder than his words.*

Free Ice Cream Marketing

"Advertising is not marketing."
Zan Monroe

Every Thursday the ice cream truck rumbled down the gravel driveway into Cloverfield Tennis and Swim Club to deliver a week's supply of ice cream to the Snack Shack at the pool. Some weeks we sold all the ice cream, while other weeks we didn't sell any ice cream at all. I watched the ice cream sales and tried to find the reason why some weeks we sold more than others. The more ice cream you sell the more profit you make, so I was interested in selling as much ice cream as possible.

Mother was at the pool one day when the ice cream truck came and we discussed the sale of ice cream. Mother waited till the delivery had been made and said, "Give some ice cream away and you will sell more."

My response was, "What? Have you lost your mind? Give away free ice cream? There goes all my profits. I would lose money on the ice cream sales for this week."

"Well, if you want to sell more ice cream, you will have to give some away," she replied, and went off to mow the lawn.

I thought about her free ice cream idea for a few days and on the following Tuesday, I discovered that we had sold almost no ice cream that week. "Give some away," I told Alice Rose Patterson, the lifeguard working in the Snack Shack. Later in the day, she called back to say we had sold out of ice cream.

When I asked Mother how she knew we would sell more ice cream if we gave some away she answered, "Have you ever seen anyone eat ice cream on a hot summer day? It looks so delightfully refreshing that you want some, too. When people see others enjoying ice cream, they will want some. Giving something away creates desire. You make up the loss by selling much more."

Mother was right, as usual. Giving free ice cream became our weekly ritual when sales were slow. When I began other businesses, I realized that ice cream marketing worked in any business. A sample of your product or service given freely will allow people to experience what you have to offer and allows others to see them enjoying it. I learned free ice cream marketing at the swimming pool.

> *"Advertising is not marketing."*
> Zan Monroe

Advertising is not marketing. Advertising is spending money in media. Marketing is understanding your client's and customer's wants and needs, and then providing products and services that satisfy those needs. Advertising attracts new customers to your business, but it is a very expensive way to grow a business.

Marketing creates repeat and referral clients because it delivers something they value. Advertising requires you to spend money. Marketing requires you to build a relationship with your customers and clients. It takes effort on your part to create, build and maintain customer relationships. Remember, you will get out of that relationship exactly what you put into it.

183

Many businesses use the principle of Free Ice Cream Marketing that Mother told me about. Detergent, software, video games – all give free samples. The current internet business model is to give people free access to the basic version of your product or service and charge for the advanced version.

Do you want to sell more of your products or services? Give some away for free and see how fast your sales increase. The next time you are outside on a hot summer day and see someone eating ice cream, try to resist the temptation to get some for yourself. Mother's principle of free ice cream marketing is betting that you cannot resist.

The Blackbird Theory of Business

"The universe is too complex to be random."
Zan Monroe

In December, the North Carolina sky turns grey and high thin-clouds signal the start of winter. The leaves are gone from the trees and the air has a damp chill that makes you cold right to your bones. It was not a good time to work in the yard, but a great time to go hunting. I loved taking the dog and my shotgun to wander around in the woods. I don't remember shooting much, but I do remember seeing a lot of deer, possum, raccoon and squirrels moving about in the woods. Geese, ducks, doves, hawks and buzzards flew overhead, as well as huge flocks of blackbirds.

Blackbirds flew south for the winter, passing overhead in giant trails that went on for minutes at a time. I liked to stop and watch them as they passed, listening to them chirp as they flew. They moved like a school of fish in the air, swirling and banking to follow an unknown leader. Occasionally, the entire flock would land in a tree or on the front lawn. They would suddenly become very quiet, and then as one body, they would lift off to fly around together for a few seconds and then relight. I tried for years to identify the leader of the flock, but it was impossible to determine. They just seemed to follow each other for no reason at all, simply going where every other blackbird went, without thinking independently for themselves.

When I asked Mother about the blackbirds she said, "There is no leader of a flock of blackbirds; they just follow the flock.

People are a lot like blackbirds. They follow the crowd and don't think for themselves. If they see others doing something, then they will want to do it, too. If you want to be successful in business, then study blackbirds. When you understand the flock mentality of blackbirds, you will understand the flock mentality of people. *The universe is too complex to be random.*

Over the years, I have studied flocks of humans and their behavior patterns, and I have determined that the universe is too complex to be random. I have reached a theory that explains the behavior of people. I call it the *Blackbird Theory of Business.*

In high school, I worked at a gas station on Interstate 95. I would sit there for hours and have no customers. Then one car would pull off the interstate into my gas station and for the next two hours I would have so many cars that I could not keep up with everyone. When one car took the exit ramp, the others checked their gas gage and did the same thing, thinking their actions were self-directed, when they were simply acting like blackbirds following the flock. The flock of cars had landed at my station. People were following what other people did without thinking about it. Then, just like a flock of blackbirds that fly away from a sweet gum tree, all the cars would be gone at the same time.

When I was in the swimming pool business, there were gorgeous summer days where no one would come to the pool. The flock had gone somewhere else. There were cold rainy days where the pool was packed with people. The flock had descended on the pool.

186

In my real estate business, I would work week after week without selling anything. The flock was not buying. Then suddenly I would sell three or four houses in the same week. The flock had arrived. When an offer came in on one house, you simply had to wait a few hours and another offer would appear on the same house. After thirty years of observing human behavior, I know it is the Blackbird Theory of Business at work.

Most people follow the crowd and will do what everyone else is doing. If everyone is buying houses, everyone else will buy houses. Between the years 2000 - 2006 was the largest, longest, strongest real estate boom in the history of mankind. It was also the worst time in history to purchase a home. There were rapidly rising prices, multiple offers and bidding wars that caused prices to go above what rational buyers should have paid. The flock had arrived. Everyone was buying houses, so everybody else bought houses.

> *"The universe is too complex to be random."*
> Zan Monroe

From 2007 - 2011 was the best time in history to purchase a house – the lowest interest rates in history, falling prices and lots of houses to choose from with no competition from other buyers. The flock had gone somewhere else. No one was buying houses because no one else was buying houses.

My advice to my business clients is to study the habits of their customers so they are prepared for them when they arrive. The flock may arrive at certain times of the day, like in restaurants or hotels. Your business may fluctuate with the day of the week, like banks or movie theaters. Your business may increase at certain times of the month, like banks and grocery stores. Your business may increase during certain months of the year, like beach resorts or snow ski areas. It is up to you to observe the patterns of your customers and be ready for your flock when they arrive.

When the flock of customers has gone, it is time to prepare your business for their return. When your business is slow, do the menial, laborious and time consuming work to get ready. Meet with your accountant, read a book and train your staff. Get ready for the rush when customers descend on you. A successful restaurant does not wait until the customer is sitting at the table to order groceries, roll silverware, or chop the onions. This should be done in anticipation of the customer's arrival. If your business does not prepare, you will not be ready to serve your customers when they return.

I hired a REALTOR® named Betty Wilson who worked for months in a neighborhood called Deerfield without any sales. One day, she called to tell me she sold two houses on the same day and would take the rest of the week off. I explained the Blackbird Theory of Business to her, and she reluctantly went back to work and sold another house that day. Now she really wanted to take a week off, but I would not let her stop. A flock of customers had descended on her neighborhood and because we recognized it, she stayed on the job every day for the next two weeks. She sold thirteen houses in next eleven days. If she had taken time off after selling the first two houses, she would have missed earning eighty thousand in eleven days. She would have missed her flock of buyers. The Blackbird Theory of Business worked again.

188

The universe is too complex to be random.

Watch for the blackbirds in your life and business. When one sale occurs, many more are just around the corner. Gear up and prepare to be inundated by the flock of people coming your way. When the flock leaves, stop worrying over where your customers have gone; they will come back in full force soon, and you should be preparing now for their arrival.

As I write this piece on the Blackbird Theory of Business, it is December, and I am at Topsail Beach, North Carolina staying at my friend David and Teresa Evans' house. A flock of black birds just descended on the power lines, yards and rooftops surrounding me, chirping and flying around. They came, I assume, to check the accuracy of my story and to remind me that *the universe is too complex to be random.*

Fertilize Before the Rain

"The perfect storm never lasts very long."
Zan Monroe

The rumbling clouds bringing the rain were closing in from the west and it was time to take shelter. The horses drifted toward the protection of the barn. Our dog, Barky, was waiting for the storm on his towel in his corner of the carport. The birds had quit flying and the leaves of the trees were twisting and showing their underside. Everyone and everything had taken shelter from the imminent storm, except Mother. She was fertilizing the lawn. There she was, with a bucket in one hand, throwing fertilizer in every direction, trying to beat the rain that was coming at any moment. We would shout, "Mama, there is a storm coming. You've got to get in the house."

"I've got to get this done before the rains come. If I fertilize before the rain, the lawn will get the nutrients immediately. The fertilizer will distribute evenly, and within a day or two our lawn will be a brilliant, healthy shade of green."

There are always storms in life, and you must fertilize before the rain starts. Prepare yourself for what is ahead and you will come out of the storm healthy and growing. A perfect storm doesn't last very long.

Use slow times in business and life to study and improve your skills. In the winter while nothing was growing or needing attention, Mother spent time sharpening the hoe, patching the wheel-

190

barrow tire, reviewing the seed catalogues or mulching leaves in the compost pile. When business slows, the successful people turn to education, books and classes to "sharpen their skills." Attend classes and change your products or services so you will be ready after the storm.

During the last slow time in my business, we studied our business model. I studied economic forecasts and researched into consumer behavior. We discovered that today's consumer behaves differently than they did just a few years ago. We began to see the big picture of the future of our industry. Then it became simple to get in front of the inevitable changes that were coming our way.

We redefined the business we were in. I thought I was in the speaking business, but we discovered that I am in the business of distributing information that helps people live a better life. We discovered that because of the changing consumer demands, our business had changed. We refocused on the most productive areas of our business and discontinued the non-profitable areas. When the economy turned around, our business exploded.

When everyone else is inside staying out of the rain, you should go out and fertilize your lawn, because a perfect storm doesn't last very long.

Watering Holly Bushes

"There are only a certain number of products
that will sell in any given market,
in any given period of time."
Zan Monroe

One of my summer jobs was to water the holly bushes that Mother and I planted down our seven hundred foot long driveway. It was too far away from the house for a garden hose to reach, so I filled gallon jugs with water and carried them to the bushes in the little beige trailer that hooked behind the riding lawn mower.

Watering bushes is boring. The only interesting thing was when I put water on the rich black soil at the base of the bush; it made the dirt look like chocolate cake batter.

As Mother helped me water the holly bushes she explained, "Simply pouring water on the ground around the bush is not enough. A plant can absorb only a certain amount of water in a given amount of time. Pour slowly and allow the soil to soak up the water at the base of the plant. If you exceed the absorption rate of the earth, the water will run off and be wasted. You have to pour water in just the right amounts over the right amount of time to allow the soil to absorb the water and feed the plant. The lesson here is to always be aware of the demand for water and supply what the plant needs. Either extreme of an oversupply or undersupply of water is not good for the plant."

Keeping the bushes watered became one of my many jobs that summer, and over time, I became an expert in the absorption rate of water on a newly planted holly bush. If you put too much water on a bush, the extra water runs off wasted and has no value to the plant. If there is not enough water to satisfy the demand of the bush, then every drop of water becomes precious, and its value goes up. Watering holly bushes gave me a great understanding of demand and supply.

Over time I have learned that calculating the Absorption Rate of markets is exactly the same as calculating the absorption rate of water on a holly bush. When there is too much of a product or service, the value (price) will go down. When there is a demand for a product or service that overwhelms supply, the value (price) must go up. All free markets seek a balance of demand and supply over time. That is how a free market works.

Absorption Rate works on any product in a free market: houses, cars, vacuum cleaners or water on holly bushes. You can calculate the absorption rate of book sales, candy or shovels. Every business in the free market has to constantly control its supply to match demand. Too much supply will cause prices to fall. Too little supply will cause prices to rise and generate competition.

Consumer demand drives the free market. Just like a holly bush demands a certain amount of water, consumers have demands they make on the free market. Demand comes first, and then supply satisfies the demand. If your business supplies a product that nobody wants, you will fail. When a business supplies a product or service that satisfies a consumer demand, that business becomes successful. A successful business determines demand and finds a way to supply it to the customer. Mother always said, "To be successful, study what people want and then find a way to supply it."

Today, I am one of the world's leading experts in Absorption Rate Analysis in the housing industry. Absorption Rate is a simple calculation to determine the rate at which houses will be sold (absorbed) over a given period of time. Absorption Rate is a calculation of supply and demand for real estate. There are only a certain number of houses that will sell in any market, in any price range, over any period of time. When the amount of houses on the market exceeds the demand, the price of houses will fall. When there are not enough houses to satisfy the demand for them, prices will rise.

> *"There are only a certain number of products that will sell in any given market, in any given period of time."*
> Zan Monroe

All markets, including real estate markets, seek balance over time. Free markets will reach balance much quicker when they are left alone from government control and regulations. When I teach absorption rate to business owners, they say calculating supply and demand in their industry is so simple they don't know why they didn't figure it out themselves. Obviously, they never had to water holly bushes for Mother in the hot summer sun.

LESSON 7

Real Estate is the Only <u>REAL</u> Investment

*Mary Monroe and her granddaughter,
Kristin Hill, in front of one of the houses
she moved and restored.*

What Would You Buy With $25,000?

"Wealth flows to real estate."
Mary Monroe

"What would you buy if you had $25,000 to spend?"

Mother was always posing a 'what if' scenario to me and waiting with a smile for my answer.

"What would you buy if you had $25,000 to spend?" was today's question.

"Well, let's see. I could get a new car. I could take a trip of a lifetime around the world. I could buy a house."

I was really interested in owning a new car or taking a trip. I probably threw that part about buying a house into the conversation just to make myself look responsible to Mother.

Her answer; "If you chose the $25,000 vacation, you would have the trip of a lifetime with memories of five star hotels and first class air fare, but thirty days later, you would have no money; only memories and pictures."

"If you chose the $25,000 vehicle, you would lose 15-20% of the value of the car as soon as you drove off the dealership lot. You would ride in style for a while, but within a few short years that car would be worth $5,000 or less. You would have lost $20,000."

"If you chose the $25,000 down payment on a $100,000 house, your money would more than double in five years. Based on the average housing appreciation rate of 5-7%, (which is the average appreciation of housing in the United States over the last 20 years), that house would be worth $133,947 five years after you purchased it. Five years of mortgage payments, on your loan of $75,000, at six percent interest would have reduced your loan balance to $68,548.46. You would have reduced your debt by $6,451.54 and gained $33,947 in appreciation. The $25,000 you originally invested in this house would have returned $40,398 in five years. That is a return of 140% over five years, or 28% return each year. And you have to deduct the property taxes from income tax while you were living in the house!"

What would you choose if you had $25,000 to spend? Mother knew that *all wealth in the United States flows to real estate.* According to the U.S. Census, approximately 65 percent of Americans own their own home. It is the largest and most important investment of our lives. Research from the National Association of REALTORS® shows that 70 percent of Americans see buying a home as the best investment they can make, while only 38 percent see their individual retirement account (IRA) as a good investment. *Only 10 percent of Americans have substantial money invested in the stock market.*

The Census also tells us that 33% of the houses in the United States are paid for free and clear. Remember when you drive to work tomorrow, every third house you pass has no mortgage.

As a nation, we hold our wealth in the equity of our homes.

Equity is the difference between what your home is worth and what you owe on it. Each month when you make your house payment, a portion of that payment will go to pay off the principle mortgage amount. Paying your monthly house payment is just like adding money to a savings account. That savings account is your home equity.

Here are seven good reasons to own your own home:

1. **Pride of Ownership** - is the number one reason people purchase a home. You can paint the walls any color you desire, turn up the volume on your music, attach permanent fixtures and decorate your home according to your taste.

> **"Wealth flows to real estate."**
> Mary Monroe

Home ownership gives your family stability and security. You are investing in the future of your family and your community.

2. **Appreciation** - Over the last 20 years, real estate has had an average appreciation of 5-7% per year.

3. **Mortgage Reduction Builds Equity** - Part of your monthly mortgage payment is applied to the principal balance of your loan which reduces the amount you owe. Consider this as a self-imposed savings program. You are saving money each month in the equity of your house. Making your monthly payment builds financial self-discipline.

4. **Payoff Your Home Mortgage Early** - You can accelerate the payoff of your mortgage by adding additional money to your

payment every month. You can pay off a 30 year, $100,000 fixed rate loan at six percent interest in only 17 years by adding just $100 per month to your monthly mortgage principal payment.

5. **Mortgage Interest Deduction** - The interest you pay on your mortgage is deductible on your income tax return in the United States.

6. **Property Tax Deduction** - Property taxes paid on your home are deductible for income tax purposes in the United States.

7. **Capital Gain Exclusion** - You can sell your personal residence if you have lived in your home two of the past five years and keep the profit free from taxation up to $250,000 for an individual, or $500,000 for a married couple filing jointly, in the United States. You can sell your house every two years subject to these limitations. You do not have to buy a replacement home or move up in value. There is no house age restriction for this tax exclusion.

8. **Preferential Tax Treatment** - If you receive more profit than the $250,000/$500,000 allowable exclusion on the sale of your home, that profit will be considered a capital asset and receive a lower tax rate than ordinary income in the United States.

Every couple of years, my sister Cornelia buys a new house. She fixes it up just the way she wants and lives happily. When she gets bored living in this house, she sells it and buys another one. She uses the tax laws to her benefit because the profit she makes from the sale of her principal residence is tax sheltered. She is able to make tax free money because she likes to buy, fix up and sell her house every couple of years.

When her daughter, Katherine, was in the third grade, her science teacher discussed the possibility of living on Mars. Katherine told her teacher, "Don't tell my mom. She will want to sell our house and move us to Mars!"

Moving your family every couple of years may not be your idea of fun, but if you like moving and fixing up houses, then consider the sale of your house a tax-free profit center within the limitations above.

Do you own your home? If not, start planning today. If you already own your home, consider the benefits of reducing your debt by adding money to your payment every month to pay off the mortgage as soon as you can.

If your home were paid for, how would it make you feel? What would your lifestyle would be like? Remember that 1/3 of all homes in the United States are paid for free and clear. When you purchase a home, you will be able to benefit from the seven good reasons for home ownership.

Remember, Mother says, *"All wealth flows to real estate."*

Money Does Grow on Trees

"Growing wealth is like growing a tree;
it is simple, but it takes time."
Mary Monroe

It was a cool fall day and the dog and I were lying in the back yard under the giant water oak tree watching the leaves rain down. That giant oak tree's trunk was six feet in diameter, and it had millions of leaves and thousands of acorns.

Somehow Mother found me and the dog.

"Stop wasting time playing with the dog and rake some leaves. Time for you to earn some money."

"Awww, Ma! I don't want to work and earn money. Why doesn't money just grow on trees?"

Mother said with a twinkle in her eye, "Money does grow on trees. Trees grow leaves, and if you rake them, I will pay you!"

Our playtime under that tree was over, and the dog looked sad. I began to rake leaves, angry and upset with Mother; but, as I thought about what she said, it began to make sense.

Money does grow on trees just like the leaves on that giant oak tree. An oak tree must build roots, trunk, branches, leaves and store enough food for itself to grow big and strong. Once the tree matures, it will produce acorns. Growing wealth is just like growing an oak tree. When you invest your money, it will grow like an oak tree from weak and fragile to sturdy and strong. You have to plant the acorns of wealth and watch your money grow.

The key to financial independence is to spend less money than you earn and invest the rest into growing Your Money Tree®.

- The steady income you earn from a job or business is the root of Your Money Tree®. That income feeds your financial tree and enables it to grow.

- Your Money Tree® grows stronger when you insure what you cannot pay for. Purchase life and health insurance to create a financial safety net.

- The trunk of Your Money Tree® is your savings. You should have enough money to cover your living expenses for at least six months. Six months of savings will allow you to live comfortably in case your income is cut off by losing a job, or by a slow month in your business. *Income is variable, but expenses and debt are constant.* Building this reserve gives you peace of mind and allows Your Money Tree® to get stronger.

"Growing wealth is like growing a tree;. it is simple, but it takes time."
Mary Monroe

- The first strong branch on Your Money Tree® is grown by opening a Profit Sharing Plan or Individual Retirement Plan. This plan will allow you to shelter income from taxes. Taxes are your largest expense each year, totaling about thirty percent of your income.

- As Your Money Tree® matures, it will begin to bear fruit. The first fruit should be the purchase of a personal residence. Find a house that is well within your budget. Make as large a down payment as you can afford. Your monthly payment, including principle, interest, taxes and insurance (PITI), should not exceed twenty five percent of your monthly income.

• As Your Money Tree® grows stronger, you should acquire residential rental properties to provide a harvest. Purchase single-family houses, townhouses, and condos, and rent them to create a stream of income. There is no greater investment in the world than owning residential rental properties that are *paid for free and clear of debt.*

Mother was right, money does grow on trees. Plant Your Money Tree® and watch your wealth grow. Start at the roots with a great job, or open a business. Build the trunk strong with a six-month savings account and tax sheltered retirement plan. Begin to harvest the fruit of Your Money Tree® when you purchase a home, and then build financial security by investing in rental property.

Remember what Mother said, *"Growing wealth is like growing a tree; it is simple, but it takes time."*

Moving a House

"Your passion must exceed your fear."
Zan Monroe

Mother grew up during the Depression and learned to reuse everything. She was great at taking old things and repurposing them. She recycled jars, rubber bands and aluminum foil. She reused her old panty hose to tie up tomato bushes in the garden. Our kitchen table is a hardwood pine, Lazy Susan table. She bought it for $20 in the mountains of North Carolina, refinished it by removing seven layers of paint, and now it is a family heirloom.

Mother always asked herself, "How can I re-use this?" No one should have been surprised when she said, "Why don't I recycle a house?"

In today's "green" society, it is fashionable to conserve resources, but no one was "greener" than my Mother; she recycled houses! Mother loved houses and decided that a great way to generate income would be to move, renovate and rent houses.

Mother's first attempt at moving houses was the corncrib on the hill beside the old tenant house. A corncrib is a small log house similar to a log cabin, but without any chinking between the logs to allow corn to be stored and dried. After the tenant house burned, Mother had my Uncle Don and his construction crew move the corncrib to her back yard.

206

After the corn crib was moved, I spent many summer nights sleeping in it on an old army cot. I spent many afternoons trying to hit bumblebees that hovered around that corncrib with a tobacco stick. I probably hit one bee in a hundred swings, but it was a fabulous game for a boy to play.

After Mother moved the corncrib, she knew that moving an entire house would be just as easy. Everything you do in life prepares you to do something else, as long as you are not afraid. She knew that your passion must exceed your fear.

Initially, Mother only wanted to provide housing for her family. One of her daughters needed a new house, so Mother concocted a scheme to sell her house to one daughter, have that daughter sell her house to her sister, and Mother move into a house she moved onto our farm and renovated. It was like musical chairs, only using houses. Her scheme worked and everyone got a new house.

The first house that Mother moved was the old Williford house located behind Tranquil Acres neighborhood. The house had been abandoned for years, and she moved it about four miles to our farm. When Mother finished rebuilding the Williford house, it appraised for twice what she spent on it. She doubled her money by moving and fixing up the old house. Doubling your money is not a bad investment, and she had a house that was an architectural showplace when she finished.

Eventually, Mother moved three more houses onto our farm and renovated each one into a fabulous example of early American architecture. She created a little community that I nicknamed

"Monroeville." Mother put a lot of "sweat equity" into the houses; we did lots of the work ourselves. When each house was finished, it was paid for completely, without a mortgage. She lived in one and rented the others to provide herself income. Those houses produced enough money for our family to live on. Mother had solved the problem of creating income for her family by owning rental houses that paid her every month.

If you are like most people, your home is your greatest investment. A home is the largest and very best investment most people make in their lives. Here are some investment questions you should ask yourself.

1. Do you own a home?

2. How long have you owned it?

3. Has it been a good investment?

4. What would your *net worth* be like if you owned ten houses, just like the one you live in?

5. What would your *lifestyle* be like if all ten of those houses were paid for free and clear and rented to tenants?

If you think that owning investment real estate would be a good choice for you, here is the key to building wealth with investment real estate:

1. Buy quality properties with twenty to twenty-five percent

down payment.

2. Purchase positive cash flow properties. Positive cash flow means that the rent paid by the tenant covers the mortgage payment, insurance, taxes and all other expenses.

3. Have the tenant help you pay off the mortgage by using their rent to make the monthly payment.

4. Your goal is to own rental properties that are paid for free and clear. You are working to create a cash flow to you from the rent for the rest of your life.

5. If the house appreciates in value it is a bonus, but you should not purchase investment property just for the potential appreciation.

"Your passion must exceed your fear."
Zan Monroe

Many people in our community thought Mother was crazy for moving houses. It was the 1970's when women did not work side by side with the men on a construction site. Mother did. She glazed windows, cleaned doors, painted and of course, gave instructions. She restored homes of character and recycled houses for her own personal use. There was a time in her life when she would not have attempted anything that the "community" would have considered crazy, but as she grew older, she realized that her passions had to be followed and her fears swept aside. Her passion for early American architecture was more powerful than her fears of what anyone else thought.

Mother was not fearless. Actually, she was afraid of a lot of things, but she did not let that stop her. *Her passion exceeded her fear.* Mother knew that fear limits your possibilities. She taught us all that, if you pursue your passions, you can achieve anything.

I accepted Mother's lesson that *your passion must exceed your fear* at an early age. With just a few exceptions, I have spent my life doing what I am passionate about. A thirty-plus year career in real estate, development and building has led to my teaching, writing and speaking.

Did I always think I was doing the right thing? Heck no. Most of the time, I felt like I was a failure! Now, I look back and see that I failed my way to success. I can see that everything I have done in life has prepared me for the next step. I have learned to be passionate about what I am doing today and not be afraid of tomorrow. I could not have accomplished the things that I have without the experience I gained by following Mother's example.

What would you do if you knew you could not fail? What would your life be like if you followed your passions without fear? What actions are you taking to secure your financial future? Begin today by converting income into income producing real estate.

Would you invest in real estate today if you knew you were creating income for your family for the next 100 years?

Remember: *Your passion must exceed your fear.*

There is Gold in That House

"There really is gold in owning houses."
Zan Monroe

It was not the fact that a house was being towed by a truck down Highway 301, that people stopped to watch. It was the hundreds of pigeons circling the house as it traveled that fascinated everyone.

The house finally stopped moving in the side pasture of our farm beyond the horse barn. Mother was moving a two hundred year old house from Saint Pauls, North Carolina to our farm. The total move was about thirty miles.

Uncle Don and I had prepared the house for the moving company. When we removed the roof, we discovered a huge colony of pigeons living in the attic. There were hundreds of pigeons who refused to leave their home during the weeks of deconstruction. The birds wheeled and circled overhead while we worked on the house. Now, they followed their home down the highway as they waited for the house to stop moving.

As we worked to prepare the two hundred year old house to be moved, car after car stopped to ask, "Did you find the gold in that house?"

Everyone told us the same story about the house and the gold. Long ago, the house had been used as a stage coach stop. The Lowry Gang robbed the stage coach of its gold and then spent

211

the night in this house. The next morning, the sheriff arrested the entire Lowry Gang in their beds, but the gold was never found. We never did find the gold, but we did look for it! The only thing we found was a silver dollar on top of one of the floor joists under the house.

Later in life, I learned that there really is gold in owning houses. I discovered that residential rental property is the world's greatest investment. I learned that there are four returns on investment real estate that don't exist in any other investment. Here they are:

1. **Cash Flow** - cash generated by the monthly rent.

2. **Principle Reduction** - The reduction on the principle loan amount by using the rent to make the monthly payments.

3. **Appreciation** - The amount appreciation in the value of the real estate over time. In the last twenty years, housing in the United States has appreciated an average of 5 – 7% per year.

4. **Depreciation** - Depreciation is your tax savings from ownership of an investment property.

Mother's analysis of the value in a house was based on its architectural style and the cost to move and renovate it. I evaluate a house based on this Simple Investment Analysis. Read through the following analysis and determine for yourself if this analysis will work for you. I think you will find that there really is gold in owning rental houses.

Simple Investment Analysis

Address: 123 Happy Investor Lane

Purchase Price of the House: $100,000

Initial Investment: $28,000 ($25,000 Down Payment +
$3,000 Closing Costs)

Monthly Principle and Interest Payment: $ 494.96
($75,000 Loan @ 5% for 20 years)

Estimated Cash Flow

$800 Gross Monthly Rent

Less monthly expenses:

($494.96) Monthly Principal and Interest Payment

($50) Monthly Taxes

($25) Insurance

($50) Maintenance (estimated)

($80) Management Fee

$100.04 Positive Monthly Cash Flow

$1,200.48 Positive Annual Cash Flow ($100.04 x 12 Months)

Four Returns on Investment

1. **Cash Flow** $1,200.48 Annual Cash Flow divided by $28,000
Initial Investment = 4.3% Return on Investment (ROI) from
Cash Flow

1,200.48 / 28,000 = 4.3%

2. **Principal Reduction:** The first year Principal Reduction of
Mortgage Debt of $2,240.48 divided by $28,000
Initial Investment = 8% Return on Principal Reduction

2,240.48 / 28,000 = 8%

3. **Appreciation:** $100,000 House Values x 2% Appreciation (very conservative) = $2,000 Annual Appreciation divided by $28,000 Initial Investment = 7.14% Appreciation
$100,000 x 2% = $2,000 / $28,000 = 7.14%

4. **Depreciation:** A depreciation expense can be taken each year for income tax purposes in the United States. The rental income divided by the IRS allowed "useful life" of the house value (not land) is applied to your tax rate. This is how your accountant will calculate your tax savings.

Estimated 1st Year Return on Investment
   1. Cash Flow = 4.3%
   2. Principle Reduction = 8%
   3. Appreciation = 7.14%
   4. Depreciation (not calculated)
First Year Return on Investment = 19.44%
   (plus depreciation not calculated)

There is definitely gold in owning real estate as an investment when you make 19.44% return on your investment in the first year you purchase an investment property.

The pigeons never gave up and stayed with the house until the construction crews put on a new roof. Then for a few weeks the pigeons circled the house or sat on the roof trying to find a way back inside.

"There really is gold in owning houses."
Zan Monroe

Mother took a house that had been a home for pigeons and restored it to its original purpose as a home for people. It will last for another two hundred years because one woman believed that there was gold in that house.

Mother was right. *There is gold in owning houses.*

The Best Time to Plant a Shade Tree

"The best time to plant a shade tree is twenty years ago.
The second best time to plant a shade tree is, today!"
Mary Monroe

One of the houses that Mother moved to our farm and rebuilt was a two-story Civil War era home. The Federal Style house was symmetrical on the front and back with brick chimneys on both ends. It had been built 200 years ago using silver cypress trees that had been hand cut and honed into 12x14 inch floor timbers. Some of those timbers were over forty feet long and had not rotted in over two hundred years. A silver cypress tree big enough to produce a timber 40'x12"x14" long no longer exists in North Carolina.

When the home renovation was complete, it was a magnificent demonstration of reclaiming a historic structure and using it for modern convenience. It was also one of Mother's greatest investments. Mother stood in the front yard looking at that house and said, "What this home really needs is two oak trees. I can envision a time in the future, sitting on that front porch in the shade of two giant oak trees looking out over this beautiful lawn."

We went to the local nursery and Mother found two oak trees that were skinny little twigs about four feet tall. We planted the trees way out in the front yard. I thought that the trees were planted too far from the house, but Mother told me, "Wait twenty years and these twigs will become giant oaks and wrap the front of this house in shade in the summer and protect it from storms in the winter."

Mother asked me, "When do you think is the best time to plant a shade tree?"

"I guess the best time to plant a shade tree is about 20 years ago, before you wanted the shade," I replied.

"You are correct. So, when is the second best time to plant a shade tree?"

After I failed to come up with the answer, she gave it to me.

Mother as we knew her best, working in the garden

"The second best time to plant a shade tree is today. Consider the future and decide where you want the shade to be. Then plant a tree in the right spot knowing that in the future, you will be able to enjoy the shade from the mature tree. You have to wait for that tree to grow large enough to allow you to rest in its shade. Plan what the bushes and trees will look like in the future and place them accordingly. If you want to be a successful landscaper, you have to think twenty years ahead.

"Landscapers who did not plan for the future will plant trees or bushes that look good today, but in a few years, they will block the house from view. If you plant just for today, without regard for the future, you will not get the results you want. A long-term plan is definitely necessary to make your landscaping efforts effective."

217

We finished planting those little oak trees in front of the house and they still seemed like frail little twigs too far out in the yard to make any difference. Mother said, "Wait twenty years and these twigs will become giant oaks and wrap the front of this house in shade in the summer and protect it from storms in the winter."

Growing wealth is like growing a shade tree; it is simple, but it takes time. The very best time to start building wealth was twenty years ago. The second best time to start building wealth is today. Start investing today and watch your investments grow over time just like an oak tree.

Before you plant a tree, you should prepare the soil. Before you can grow wealth, you should prepare your plan by determining what you want to accomplish. Begin with the long-term future in mind.

Here are some questions to ask as you begin to invest in real estate:
- Where do you want to end up financially?
- How much income do you want each month?
- How soon do you want to get there?
- What do you need to do to get started?
- What do you need to do each year to get there?
- How much money do you have to invest?
- Are you willing to work a second job, living on the income from one job and investing the income from the second?
- Can you borrow against existing properties, sell a car, house or stocks to buy additional properties?
- How much debt are you comfortable with?
- How much time are you willing to spend to find, buy and manage properties?

- Are you handy with tools, or do you prefer to hire someone to do repairs?
- Do you have the time and knowledge to manage your own properties, or do you want to hire a property manager?
- Do you know a property manager you have confidence in?
- Do you have geographic stability in your job or profession?
- Can you rent and hold the property for three to five years?
- Do you prefer to own properties in your hometown or in another location?
- What type of properties are you most comfortable owning?
  a. Single Family Homes: Where?
  b. Townhomes: Where?
  c. Condos: Where?
- Aside from the economic benefits, what are your other reasons for investing in real estate?

A great way to build wealth is with residential rental property. Take a moment to answer the questions about your investment future, then create your plan for financial independence. Plant your investments in residential rental property and watch them as they grow toward a strong financial future.

It has been thirty years since Mother and I planted those fragile little oak trees way out in the front yard. I rode by the house the other day and saw that those little twigs have now grown into huge oak trees that shade the house in the summer and protect it from storms in the winter.

Mother would say, *"The best time to plant a shade tree is twenty years ago. The second best time to plant a shade tree is, today."*

Real Estate Is the Only <u>REAL</u> Investment

"The word REAL estate wipes out all other investments."
Mark Twain

When I was twenty years old, my brother-in-law and I built Cloverfield Tennis and Swim Club. I played collegiate tennis at North Carolina State University, and since high school, I had been running a summer business teaching swimming and tennis on our farm. It was a simple transition to building a large tennis and swim facility. We purchased thirteen acres of land from my Uncle Dean and Uncle Adrian and began the project.

Mother immediately said, "Oh, let me find you an old house to move, renovate and use as your club house."

We ignored Mother's old-fashioned idea and hired an architect to design the clubhouse; then we took those plans to a builder. The estimated cost to build the new structure was astronomical! Our project was dead in the water.

Mother was right there saying, "I can find you a charming old house to purchase, move and renovate as your clubhouse. It will be an architectural delight and have character, too."

It was not long before Mother's wisdom became apparent. She located the old Coy Wade home place. We purchased it and moved it to the club property. Then, we renovated that old house into a fabulous example of southern charm. Mother also helped us design the rest of the club's buildings in Williamsburg style.

220

The architecture and charm of these old houses became a focal point for people in the area to enjoy and made Cloverfield Tennis and Swim Club something special.

Our local newspaper at the time, *The Fayetteville Observer,* discovered what Mother was doing and interviewed her about moving, renovating and preserving early American homes. They published a huge article on her, featuring her homes and the tennis and swim club facility, which helped us gain new members.

Mother knew how to invest in real estate. She knew that Mark Twain was right when he said, *"The word REAL estate wipes out all other investments."*

Here are the steps you should take before you begin to invest in residential real estate:

1. Set your investment goals and determine what you want.
2. Determine exactly what your perfect rental property would be and pursue only that type of property.
3. Owning residential rental property is a business, and you should treat it like one. Talk to your accountant and/or tax attorney and ask about the benefits of setting up a Profit Sharing Plan or a Limited Liability Company to own the investment real estate.
4. Meet with your local lender and get pre-approved for loans.
5. Find a qualified REALTOR® to help you purchase your investment property. Make sure they have knowledge of the investment market and a personality you can work with.
6. Select your property manager, if you are going to use one.

7. Use standard leases, application forms and credit checks. Your REALTOR® can help you with this.
8. Set up your files and bookkeeping system for each property.
9. Make a list of trusted service contractors for heating and air conditioning, plumbing, electrical, roofing and construction.

Cloverfield Tennis and Swim Club was successful both as a business and as an investment in real estate. The business lessons I learned while operating the club were invaluable in my later life. I also developed the land into a neighborhood, sold the home sites and built houses. It was only logical that I built and developed houses because that is what Mother taught us to do. I learned that real estate was my true calling and it has been my focus for the rest of my life.

While I cannot recommend moving houses as a way to invest in real estate, owning real estate is one of the very best investments that exists today. Begin today, to work toward your goal of financial independence.

Remember what Mark Twain said, *"The word REAL estate, wipes out all other investments."*

Tax Sheltered Real Estate Investments

*"The only money that you put in the stock market
is money you are willing to lose."*
Mary Monroe

Mother's generation had a saying, *"The only money that you put in the stock market is money you are willing to lose."* Mother was a teenager when the Great Depression hit in 1927. She always remembered the stock market crashed and people lost their entire savings overnight. Today, we are encouraged by our tax laws, accountants and stock brokers to gamble our money into the roulette wheel of the stock market. They tell us that our money will be safe, and if you put enough money in, you will be able to retire at age sixty-five. Most of us still remember what Mother said, *"The only money that you put in the stock market is money you're willing to lose."*

Another reason Mother did not put money into the stock market was she simply did not understand it. Neither do I. Over the last fifteen years, I have sat in monthly financial meetings with a stock broker explaining the investments one of my businesses has in the stock market. They use terms I don't understand with diagrams and graphs that mean very little to me. Our investments have done extremely well, but I simply don't understand how the stock market works.

Mother understood real estate. So do you and I. You understand real estate because you live in it every day. After years of studying and searching, I have learned that you can own real estate investments in a tax sheltered Profit Sharing Plan. Mother would have loved to have known how to do that.

The Internal Revenue Service regulates the use of Retirement Plans. Their rules are really, very simple. Your Retirement Plan is an account that allows your money to be invested without tax on the gains your investments make until you take the money out of the account. The IRS has rules about how and where the money in that account can be invested, which include stocks, bonds, mutual funds *and real estate.* Your stock broker has never told you about real estate because they deal in stocks, bonds and mutual funds and not real estate. Most stock brokers don't understand real estate and most REALTORS® don't understand tax sheltered investments. When it comes to tax sheltered investing in real estate, you have to do your own research. Here are my recommendations:

• Talk to your CPA and a *knowledgeable* tax attorney to see if owning investment real estate in a tax sheltered Profit Sharing Plan is right for you.

• To qualify for a Profit Sharing Plan, you will need to own a business or be an independent contractor. If you are an employee, consider a Self-Directed IRA which can do the same thing, but has much higher fee.

• If your business has employees, review your legal requirements for contributions to the Profit Sharing Plan with your CPA or tax attorney.

- Your tax attorney will set up the Profit Sharing Plan.

- Your Profit Sharing Plan will have a Tax ID number that per-forms the same function as an individual Social Security Number. This Tax ID number is simply a way for the IRS to track the activ-ities of your plan. There will be yearly tax returns and reporting to the IRS.

- Use the Tax ID number to set up a regular checking account at your local bank in the name of your Profit Sharing Plan.

- You make contributions to your Profit Sharing Plan just like any other retirement account. The more income you make, the more you can contribute. You can shelter huge amounts of money in a Profit Shar-

> *"The only money that you put in the stock market is money you are willing to lose."*
> Mary Monroe

ing Plan as compared to other Retirement Plans. Your accountant will assist you in determining the amounts you can contribute.

- You can transfer money from your current Individual Retire-ment Plan into your Profit Sharing Plan.

- Once your Profit Sharing Plan is set up, it can then purchase in-vestment real estate. The deed to the property will be made in the name of your Profit Sharing Plan. All rents are paid to the Profit Sharing Plan and all operating expenses for the property are paid from the Profit Sharing Plan.

- There are rules to operating your Profit Sharing Plan that your tax attorney and accountant will review with you, but here are the basics:

- You will be the trustee of the plan and have complete control and responsibility for all record keeping.

- You will have complete control over the investments of the plan.

- Never use property owned by the Profit Sharing Plan for family or personal use.

- Don't buy or sell real estate in the Profit Sharing Plan with family members.

- Do not move real estate previously owned by you as an individual into the Profit Sharing Plan without the advice of your CPA or tax attorney.

- Never co-mingle personal funds with Profit Sharing Plan money. If the IRS determines that you have co-mingled funds, you will lose the tax benefits and pay huge penalties.

- If your Profit Sharing Plan borrows money, it will be a portfolio loan from a commercial bank. You will not get any government backed loans (FHA, VA, Fannie Mae and Freddie Mac) for Profit Sharing Plans. You cannot personally guarantee a loan for your Profit Sharing Plan.

Do you believe that you are capable of investing your money to create financial independence, or do you believe that job should be turned over to a stock broker? If you think you're smart enough to guide your own financial future, then you should look into your own Profit Sharing Plan.

Investing in real estate is a great idea. Investing in real estate in a tax sheltered Profit Sharing Plan is a fabulous way to build wealth rapidly without paying taxes until later in life. If you want a retirement plan that works, then I urge you to look into owning tax sheltered real estate.

Remember what Mother's generation said, *"The only money that you put in the stock market is money you're willing to lose."*

Did They Get It?

Mother asked me, "What do you want to do with your life?"

I told her that I wanted to travel the world and teach the lessons she had taught me. That mission is still the driving force behind my speaking, writing and teaching today. The reason I wrote this book is to share Mother's philosophy in life and business.

Toward the end of Mother's life, I was booked to speak in Las Vegas at a large company's international convention. She helped me create a presentation that covered a great deal of the information in this book. Part of the presentation was about the three factors that make a person complete: *Reason, Purpose and Self-Esteem. Reason* is the ability to think. Your mind is your only tool of survival. *Purpose* is to have creative, productive work as the standard of your life. *Sel-Esteem* is to know you are worthy of living a life of joy, prosperity and happiness.

Mother was admitted into the hospital a few days prior to my departure for the Las Vegas presentation. My sisters agreed I should do the presentation because Mother had helped me prepare it. She would want me to deliver her message and not stay at her bedside.

At the Las Vegas convention, the opening keynote speaker was Dr. Phil. I spoke next, and as I spoke, the room filled with more and more people until there was standing room only. There were people sitting on the floor who refused to move even when the fire marshal came and ordered them out. Those people wanted to hear

Mother's message.

After the presentation, I rushed home to see Mother in the hospital. She had not spoken in several days and she was asleep when I arrived. When she awoke, I began to describe the presentation and how the audience responded to the message that she helped develop. I explained how the room had been packed with more people than there were seats; how some people were standing and many simply sat on the floor for the entire presentation.

She smiled and then patted my hand to make me be quiet, She asked quietly, "Did they get it?"

The only thing she wanted to know about the presentation was, did the audience get the message she and I were trying to convey? Did they understand the importance of the message? Did they absorb and assimilate the message into their lives? She wanted to know if they understood and responded to *her message delivered by me.*

She smiled and went back to sleep. A couple of weeks later, at midnight, on March 26, 2003, Mother passed away just as she wanted... comfortable in her bed at her home with the fragrant smell of early spring flowers in the room, never to have spoken again.

"Did they get it?" was the last thing she ever said to me.

After reading this book, Mother would ask you one question: "Did you get it?"

Mother would be pleased if your answer is, YES!

Appendix

Mary Monroe's Reading List

As a Man Thinketh - James Allen
The Power of Positive Thinking - Norman Vincent Peale
How to Win Friends and Influence People - Dale Carnegie
Success through a Positive Mental Attitude - Napoleon Hill
   and W. Clement Stone
The Richest Man in Babylon - George S. Clason
The Greatest Salesman in the World - Og Mandino
Think and Grow Rich/The Law of Success - Napoleon Hill
The Psychology of Self Esteem/Six Pillars of Self Esteem/
Breaking Free/Honoring the Self/The Disowned Self
   - Nathanial Brandon
Capitalism and Freedom - Milton Friedman
Rich Dad Poor Dad (all his books) - Robert T. Kiyosaki
The One Minute Manager - Kenneth Blanchard
Who Moved My Cheese? - Dr. Spencer Johnson

Everything Ayn Rand wrote:
Novels: *Anthem/The Fountainhead/Atlas Shrugged/Night*
   of January 16th/We the Living
Non Fiction: *The Art of Fiction/The Objectivist Newsletter/*
   Capitalism: The Unknown Ideal/For the New Intellectual/
   Introduction to Objectivist Epistemology/Philosophy:
   Who Needs It/The Romantic Manifesto/The Virtue of
   Selfishness
   Objectivism: The Philosophy of Ayn Rand - Leonard Peikoff

<u>She would also read anything written by or about:</u>
Cato Institute
Heritage Foundation
Imprimis from Hillsdale College
Thomas Sowell
Ronald Reagan
Thomas Jefferson

Simple Investment Analysis

Address: 123 Happy Investor Lane
$100,000 Price
$25,000 Down payment + $ 3,000 Closing Costs = $28,000
   Initial Investment
$75,000 Loan @ 5.0% for 20 years = $494.96 Monthly P&I Pmt.

Estimated Cash Flow

$800.00 Net Monthly Rent (Gross Rent less Homeowner's Fee)
($494.96) less Monthly Principal & Interest Payment
($50.00) less Monthly Taxes
($25.00) less Insurance
($130.00) less other: Maintenance ($50) & Mgmt. ($80)
$100.04 Monthly Cash Flow x 12 = $ 1,200.48 Annual Cash Flow

Three Returns on Investment

1. Cash Flow
   $1,200.48 Annual Cash Flow/(divided by) $28,000.0 Initial
    Investment = 4.3% Cash Flow Return
2. Principal Reduction
   $2,240.48 Annual Principal/(divided by) $28,000.0 Initial
   Investment = 8% Principal Reduction
3. Appreciation at 2% (very conservative) x $100,000 value
   $2,000 Annual Appreciation/(divided by) $28,000 Initial
   Investment = 7.14% Appreciation

Estimated 1st Year Return on Investment (1+2+3) = <u>19.44%</u>

Simple Investment Analysis

Address_____

$_____ Price

$_____ Down Payment + $_____ Closing Costs =

$_____ Initial Investment

$_____ Loan @_____ % for _____ Years =

$_____ Monthly P&I Pmt.

Estimated Cash Flow

$_____ Net Monthly Rent (Gross Rent less
Homeowner's Fee)

($_____) less Monthly Principal and Interest Payment

($_____) less Monthly Taxes

($_____) less Insurance

($_____) less Other _____

$_____ Monthly Cash Flow x 12 = $_____
Annual Cash Flow

Three Returns on Investment

1. Cash Flow

$_____ Annual Cash Flow

_____ = _____ % Cash Flow Return

$_____ Initial Investment

2. Principal Reduction

$_____ Annual Principal

_____ = _____% Principal Reduction

$_____ Initial Investment

3. Appreciation @_____ %

$_____ Annual Appreciation

_____ = _____ % Appreciation

$_____ Initial Investment

Estimated 1st Year Return on Investment

(1+2+3) = _____ %

A Dragon Story

*One of the many dragon stories told by
Zan Monroe to his children at bedtime.*

Once upon a time, in a land far, far away, there lived a young prince. His name was Prince Snarfblat Umberhammer *(change the name every time)*. No one in the kingdom could pronounce his name, so the just called him Prince Cameron *(substitute your child's name)*. Prince Cameron had a sister called Princess Snugglebunny Beetlewocker *(change the name every time),* but everyone just called her Princess Louisa (substitute your child's name) because it was easier. *(Use as many princes and princesses as you have children listening to the story)*.

One day a horse and rider came across the grassy plain toward the castle. He thundered across the drawbridge and up the cobblestone pathway into the courtyard with his horse's hooves echoing off the castle walls.

When his horse slid to a stop, he called for Prince Cameron and Princess Louisa. When they arrived he said, "I have grave news from the southern part of your kingdom! A dragon has invaded the land and is terrorizing the livestock and eating the peasants. *(NOT eating the livestock and terrorizing the peasants.)*

"Prince Cameron and Princess Louisa, you must save your kingdom from this terrible dragon."

Prince Cameron saddled his horse and got his sword and his

shield and his baseball and glove. *(Use whatever toy, device, or event your child is focused upon today.)*

Princess Louisa saddled her horse and got her sword and her shield and her guitar *(use whatever toy, device, or event your child is focused upon today)*. They rode their horses across the drawbridge, down the dusty dirt road, across the huge green, grassy field heading south to vanquish the dragon from their kingdom.

The first village they came to was Wedgieville. Prince Cameron and Princess Louisa were very careful not to stop and dismount from their horses in Wedgieville because the townspeople were know for sneaking up behind you, grabbing your underwear and pulling them up suddenly to create a gigantic wedgie!

Today, however, there were no worries about getting a wedgie in Wedgieville because the entire village was having a wedgie day celebration! Everyone was sporting their best wedgie pants and there was a wedgie parade marching right down Main Street led by the mayor of Wedgieville.

After Prince Cameron and Princess Louisa left Wedgieville, they went over the river and through the woods to Honey's house. *(Or whatever you call your Grandma or friend or family member where the children like to go.)*

Prince Cameron and Princess Louisa tied their horses to the fence outside of Honey's *(Grandma's)* house and went inside. Honey was busy puttering in the kitchen, fixing the most delicious smelling lunch.

Honey asked, "Where are you two going?"

"Oh, there is a terrible dragon in the southern part of our kingdom. We have to vanquish the dragon because he is eating the livestock and terrorizing the peasants" *(yes, I changed it and if your children notice then they are still wide awake!)*

"Well, before you do battle with a dragon, you better eat a good lunch," said Honey.

They sat down at the big wooden table in the kitchen and Honey served them fried chicken, butter beans, mashed potatoes and big warm rolls with butter and blackberry jelly. *(Or whatever your grandmother would fix for dinner or whatever your children would like most.)*

They ate until they could eat no more, and then went out on the front porch. Honey sat in the swing and Prince Cameron and Princess Louisa stretched out in the warm sunshine and drifted off to sleep.

(This would be a good time to check and see if your kids are still awake!)

When they woke up, they were refreshed, and said to Honey, "Thanks for the lunch, it was delicious. Now, it is time for us to go do battle with the dragon."

"What weapons did you bring with you to battle the dragon?" asked Honey.

Prince Cameron said, "I brought my sword and my shield and my baseball and glove." *(Use whatever toy, device, or event your child brought)* Princess Louisa said, "I brought my sword and my shield and my guitar." *(Use whatever toy, device, or event your child brought)*

"Oh, that will never do," said Honey. "That dragon will never be conquered by such pitiful weapons. You need some real weapons. I will give you the greatest weapons in the world.

"There is only one weapon great enough to conquer a great dragon and that is your mind! Your mind is your only tool of survival. I will give you reason, purpose and self-esteem! With these three weapons you can conquer any foe.

"Reason is the ability to think. Purpose is to have creative, productive work as the standard of your life and self esteem is to know you are worthy of living a life of joy, prosperity and happiness."

"Are you sure that these weapons will work?" they asked.

"Trust me, they are all you need to conquer any foe," said Honey.

Prince Cameron and Princess Louisa set off in search of the dragon, armed with the greatest weapons known to mankind. They went down the lane, across the creek, into the woods, up the hills, down the valleys and past the big rocks until they came to the cave where the dragon lived.

Prince Cameron dismounted his horse, walked to the mouth of the cave and drew his sword. He banged the blade of his sword on the entrance of the cave and yelled into the darkness, "This is Prince Cameron and I protect my kingdom from all invaders. I will not allow you to continue to terrorize the livestock and eat the peasants. *(Yes, it changed again)* I command you, Mr. Dragon *(sometimes it's Miss or Mrs.)* to come out so we can do battle and I can vanquish you from my kingdom!"

As Prince Cameron stepped back from the doorway, there was a rumbling deep inside the earth. The dragon had been sleeping, as dragons often do, and he (she) was not particularly happy at being awakened by the prince. The dragon emerged slowly from the mouth of the cave. First, his head appeared; as big as a car, covered with bright yellow horns and emerald green scales that glistened in the sunlight. His eyes were brilliant blue. As he emerged from the cave, Prince Cameron and Princess Louisa realized the dragon was as big as a school bus. His feet were the size of the hood of a car, and they were black with bright orange toenails.

(Each time, make the dragon different colors and a different size. There are times when the dragon is no bigger than a housecat.)

"Who wakes the great dragon?" roared the dragon.

"It is I, Prince Cameron. Prepare to do battle because I have come to stop you from terrorizing the peasants and eating the livestock." *(Changed again.)*

Prince Cameron drew his sword and his shield and the dragon attacked immediately. The dragon's body was covered in green scales that were hard as steel, and Prince Cameron's sword could not pierce them. Prince Cameron used his sword and shield as best he could, but he was no match for the dragon. Finally, with a sudden sweep of his tail, the dragon knocked Prince Cameron to the ground and stepped on him with one gigantic foot to hold him still so he could eat the young prince.

Suddenly, the dragon heard the most wonderful sound. It was the sound of Princess Louisa playing her guitar and singing. As we all know, music soothes the soul of the savage beast. Immediately, the dragon stopped trying to kill Prince Cameron and lay down at Princess Louisa's feet to listen to her beautiful songs. *(Or whatever your child brought with them on their quest.)*

She sang a song about her most powerful weapons: Reason, Purpose and Self-Esteem.

"There is no way you can defeat us because we have the most powerful weapons in the world," said Princess Louisa. "Why don't you stop fighting and join us in a day of fun?"

The dragon knew he was defeated because anyone who has Reason, Purpose and Self-Esteem cannot be defeated by anything, or anyone.

"The only reason I was terrorizing the livestock and eating the peasants is because no one would play with me," said the dragon. "Besides, peasants don't even taste good!"

Then, the dragon spied Prince Cameron's baseball and glove *(or whatever your child brought)* and asked if they could play.

So, while Princess Louisa played her guitar and sang, Prince Cameron and the dragon played baseball and had the most wonderful time. *(Use whatever your Prince and Princess brought with them to make friends with the dragon because the dragon really wants to play with these toys!)*

Finally, Prince Cameron and Princess Louisa said it was time to go home, because they had to be back at the castle before dark. The dragon volunteered to give them a ride home; so, they climbed upon his back, and with one great swoop of his wings, they were flying toward their castle.

When the dragon landed in the castle courtyard, he promised to stop terrorizing the peasants and eating the livestock and come back the next day to play. Then they all crawled in their soft, warm beds and went sound asleep. *(Your children should be asleep by now!)*

The End.

This dragon story is a tribute to the life of
Mary Cornelia Williams Monroe, who gave us all the greatest
weapon in the world: Reason, Purpose and Self-Esteem.

Zan Monroe told this dragon story in Mary Monroe's bedroom
on the last evening of her life. This story was the last thing
Mary Cornelia Williams Monroe heard.

**My mission is to inspire and educate
ten million people by January 1, 2020.**

For additional inspirational material,
including downloadable audio and print library,
to purchase products, or to learn more about
Zan Monroe, visit his website at
ZanMonroe.com

Zan Monroe
The Monroe Company, Inc.
PO Box 58241 ~ Fayetteville NC 28305
910-624-7100
Zan@ZanMonroe.com

Zan Monroe

Zan Monroe is an entrepreneur who started his first business at the age of sixteen and his first corporation at the age of twenty-one. He now oversees the operation of numerous businesses and corporations.

Zan is a writer, speaker and consultant. He has published two books, Stories of Uncle Adrian and 7 Lessons for Success. He records, writes and speaks to thousands of people each year about life mastery, business, sales, marketing, leadership and investing.

Zan's Leadership and Management coaching helps businesses raise their production and become more profitable. His events enable companies to create a clear vision of the future and develop the skills that turn talent into production. His clients include Fortune 500 companies in the real estate, banking, mortgage, building, insurance and title industries, as well as the public.

Zan travels the world serving the needs of his clients, but his heart is with his family in his hometown of Fayetteville, NC.

Made in the USA
Lexington, KY
06 January 2019